PRACTICAL THEOLOGY

Practical Theology

Edited, with an Introduction, by

DON S. BROWNING

1817

Harper & Row, Publishers, San Francisco
Cambridge, Hagerstown, New York, Philadelphia
London, Mexico City, São Paulo, Sydney

FIRST EDITION

Designer: Jim Mennick

Library of Congress Cataloging in Publication Data
Main entry under title:

PRACTICAL THEOLOGY.

   Includes index.
   Contents: The foundation of practical theology / Don Browning—Theology and practice outside the clerical paradigm / Edward Farley—Schleiermacher's vision for theology / John Burkhart—[etc.]
   1. Theology, Practical—Addresses, essays, lectures. I. Browning, Don S.
BV3.P69   1983   230   82–47739
ISBN 0–06–061153–7

83 84 85 86 87   10 9 8 7 6 5 4 3 2 1

To My Teachers

SEWARD HILTNER
PERRY LEFEVRE
BERNARD LOOMER

Contents

Contributors

DON S. BROWNING is Alexander Campbell Professor of Religion and Psychological Studies at the Divinity School of the University of Chicago, where he is also Dean of the Disciples Divinity House. He is the author of *The Moral Context of Pastoral Care* and *Pluralism and Personality: William James and Some Contemporary Cultures of Psychology*.

JOHN E. BURKHART is Professor of Systematic Theology at McCormick Theological Seminary. He is the author of *Worship*.

EDWARD FARLEY, Professor of Theology at the Divinity School of Vanderbilt University, is the author of *Ecclesial Man: A Social Phenomenology of Faith and Reality* and *Ecclesial Reflection: An Anatomy of Theological Method*.

JAMES W. FOWLER is Professor of Theology and Human Development and Director of the Center for Faith Development at Candler School of Theology, Emory University. He is the author of *Stages of Faith: The Psychology of Human Development and the Quest for Meaning* and, with Sam Keen, *Life Maps: Conversations on the Journey of Faith*.

LEANDER E. KECK, Dean of Yale Divinity School and Winkley Professor of Biblical Theology at Yale, is the author of *A Future for the Historical Jesus* and *The Bible in the Pulpit*.

JAMES N. LAPSLEY is Carl and Helen Egner Professor of Pastoral Theology at Princeton Theological Seminary. He is the editor of *The Concept of Willing* and the author of *Salvation and Health*.

DENNIS P. MCCANN is Assistant Professor of Religious Studies at De Paul University. He is the author of *Christian Realism and Liberation Theology: Practical Theologies in Creative Con-*

flict and, with Charles Strain, *The New Messiah? A Future for Practical Theology* (forthcoming).

THOMAS W. OGLETREE, Dean and Professor of Theological Ethics at the Theological School, Drew University, is the author of *The Death of God Controversy* and the editor, with George R. Lucas, of *Lifeboat Ethics.*

DAVID TRACY is Professor of Theology at the Divinity School of the University of Chicago and the author of *Blessed Rage for Order: The New Pluralism in Theology* and *The Analogical Imagination: Christian Theology and the Culture of Pluralism.*

Acknowledgments

APPRECIATION needs to be expressed to the following individuals and organizations who helped make this volume possible. First, the deepest thanks need to be paid to Robert Lynn and the Lilly Endowment for the generous grant that largely made possible the conference at which earlier versions of six of the chapters contained in this volume were presented in lecture form. Gratitude also needs to be expressed to the administrators of the William Henry Hoover Lectures on Christian Unity of the Disciples Divinity House of the University of Chicago who had the vision to see that an interfaith conference on practical theology would, in its own way, make a unique contribution to ecumenical progress. Appreciation needs to go to Dean Franklin Gamwell of the Divinity School of the University of Chicago and Martin Marty, Director of the Institute for the Advanced Study of Religion, for convening the original conference entitled "Theology and Practice: Ecumenical Perspectives on Practical Theology," which was held in January 1981. I want to thank Bernie Lyon and Mark Taylor, who, in their capacity as Junior Fellows of the Institute for the Advanced Study of Religion, assisted me in coordinating the conference and the six-month seminar that followed it. Mr. Lyon also prepared the index. And finally, I want to indicate my appreciation for the generous support displayed by John Shopp of Harper & Row throughout the preparation of this book.

DON S. BROWNING

1. Introduction

DON S. BROWNING

SIX OF the chapters in this volume were first delivered as lectures at a major conference held at the Divinity School of the University of Chicago in January of 1981. This conference was convened by the Divinity School's Institute for the Advanced Study of Religion but underwritten by the William Henry Hoover Lectures on Christian Unity of the Disciples Divinity House at Chicago and a particularly generous grant from the Lilly Endowment. The remaining three chapters were not given at the original conference but are included because for various reasons they are relevant to the concerns of this volume.

The conference grew out of conversations with my colleagues at the Divinity School, especially Dean Chris Gamwell, James Gustafson, David Tracy, Robin Lovin, and Martin Marty. Over the last three years or so, it seemed that the phrase "practical theology" was creeping into our conversations more and more. Observations made and questions asked about practical theology became more frequent. Wasn't contemporary theological education selling it short? Couldn't the areas of practical theology be better defined, better ordered? Wasn't the widespread idea entirely wrong that practical theology was "simple-minded theology" and "easy," while systematic and biblical theology was "hard" and therefore "intellectually respectable"? Wasn't it the case that practical theology appeared confused and soft-headed because it was indeed the most difficult branch of theology, requiring the widest range of theological skills and judgments, and because the challenging intellectual work needed to clarify its logic and methods had simply not been sufficiently attempted? Wasn't this failure to have a clear and vibrant approach to practical theology part of the reason that so many ministers and lay people testify to the irrelevance of contemporary theology? Is it possible that they intuitively sense that much of philosophical and systematic theology, although important, is still somehow incomplete, leaving out matters necessary to give theology a cutting edge in the world in which most of us live? In light of these questions and many others, it was decided that the newly formed Institute for the Advanced Study of Religion should hold, as one of its early public programs, a major conference on this neglected yet vital area of theology.

The Renewal of Practical Theology
The original conference participants consisted of two philosophical theologians (Professors Edward Farley and David Tracy), a social ethicist (Professor Dennis McCann), a New Testament scholar and contributor to homiletical theory (Professor Leander Keck, now Dean of Yale Divinity School), a religious educator (Professor James Fowler), and a pastoral theologian (Professor James Lapsley). The chapter by Professor John E. Burkhart on "Schleiermacher's Vision for Theological Education" was specially commissioned by a seminar on practical theology that met for six months after the conference and consisted of professors from the Chicago Cluster of Theological Schools and the Divinity School. The importance of Friedrich Schleiermacher for our vision of theological education in general and practical theology in particular emerged as an important theme at both the conference and the seminar that followed; it seemed mandatory to examine Schleiermacher more systematically, and Professor Burkhart kindly consented to prepare a special paper for our consideration. Although Professor Thomas Ogletree, now Dean of the Theological School of Drew University, did not participate in the original conference or seminar, his chapter is included because of the importance of his statement and because it illustrates the widespread new interest in reestablishing the foundations of practical theology that seems to have flowered across the land. Professor Ogletree's chapter was first delivered as a lecture before the Association for Professional Education for Ministry during the summer of 1980. It was thought helpful to include my chapter on "Pastoral Theology in a Pluralistic Age" because it is referred to by both James Lapsley and James Fowler in their

contributions to this volume. It was first delivered at a Pastoral Theology Colloquy in Honor of Seward Hiltner held at Princeton Theological Seminary in March of 1980. And finally, it should be acknowledged that it was a shortcoming of the original conference, and is a deficiency in this book, that there was not found for either an appropriate contribution on liturgics.

I point out the origin of these chapters with some care for a specific reason: I am trying to illustrate that the renewed interest in the foundations of practical theology is not confined to professors who teach practical courses in denominational seminaries. Three of the chapters are written by theologians and two by theological ethicists. Most of the chapters are written by professors teaching in university-related divinity schools, and only two of the authors actually teach in departments of practical theology. Some of the chapters originated in contexts other than the original conference.

But there is even further evidence of renewed interest in this area. We hear from the liberation theologians about theologies of praxis and theology as orthopraxis. We hear of novel ideas such as religious education as a "shared praxis" or of a "praxis approach" to pastoral care. Aristotelian, Hegelian, and Marxist ideas of praxis have strongly influenced a variety of contemporary theological movements and have given theology in general a new interest in questions of right action in addition to its traditional interests in right meaning and correct belief. There seems to be a growing hunger to make theology in general more relevant to the guidance of action and to bridge the gap between theory and practice, thought and life, the classic theological disciplines and practical theology.

New Perspectives: A Review

Before providing readers with a summary and review of the major themes running through these nine chapters, a brief review of the major thrust of each chapter may prove helpful. The volume begins with two chapters, one by Edward Farley and one by John Burkhart, that throw considerable light on the historical backgrounds to our present crisis in theological education in general and practical theology in particular.

In many ways, Edward Farley's chapter, "Theology and Practice Outside the Clerical Paradigm," sets the agenda for this volume as it did for the original conference. Although full of constructive proposals, his chapter contains a rich discussion of the history of the various forms theology has taken. It is developed around distinctions he draws between four different understandings or genres of theology: theology as *habitus,* theology as science, theology as faculty, and theology as a discrete discipline such as systematic theology. Theology as *habitus* (wisdom) emphasized an approach to understanding God that combined both existential and scientific dimensions. It cut across, Farley believes, our present dichotomies between theory and practice, systematic theology and practical theology. But since the Reformation theology as *habitus* has been replaced by theology as faculty (theology as a collection of specialized disciplines such as Bible, church history, dogmatics, practical theology) and theology as a specific discipline within this body of divinity. When theology as faculty grew to be dominant, the problem became getting the specialized disciplines back together again. Friedrich Schleiermacher, the great German pastor and theologian (1768–1834), drafted an answer to this problem to fit the needs of the German university in his classic *Kurze Darstellung des theologischen Studiums,* or *Brief Outline of the Study of Theology.* The disciplines of theology as faculty should be organized, he argued, around the professional education of ministers. Practical theology should be the crowning discipline organizing the other theological specialties toward the end of formulating the specific rules and procedures governing clerical practice in the church. This ends, according to Farley, in the unhappy captivity of practical theology to what he calls the "clerical paradigm."

John Burkhart in his chapter on Schleiermacher confirms much of Farley's sketch of Schleiermacher's solution. Schleiermacher divided the disciplines of theology into philosophical (the root), historical (the body), and practical theology (the crown). Philosophical and historical theology find their purpose and interest from practical theology (the crown). Their final *raison d'être* comes from what they contribute to the task of professional ministerial leadership and the governance of the church. But

Burkhart is clear in showing that Schleiermacher saw no other significant way for practical theology to contribute anything to the foundational disciplines of philosophical and historical theology. Hence Burkhart agrees with Farley that Schleiermacher's brilliant solution did indeed tend to reduce practical theology to a preoccupation with technique and helped create an unfortunate dichotomy between theology and practice.

The next two chapters, "The Foundations of Practical Theology" by David Tracy and "Dimensions of Practical Theology: Meaning, Action, Self" by Thomas Ogletree, are foundational attempts to state both the organization of theology and the place of practical theology within it. Before moving on to these chapters, however, I would like to point out that Farley, in addition to his historical contributions, offers constructive insights on this topic as well. For instance, he wants to reinstate the centrality of theology as *habitus* and give new substance to practical theology by organizing it around a phenomenology of "ecclesial redemptive presence." Building practical theology around a careful description of the dimensions of ecclesial presence in all of its "world transforming" character will deliver it, Farley believes, from its captivity to the clerical paradigm, that is, the skills and procedures needed by professional ministers to maintain the internal life of the church.

In his chapter on the foundations of practical theology David Tracy carries forward themes recently discussed in his well-received *Blessed Rage for Order* (1975) and *The Analogical Imagination* (1981).[1] Tracy employs his revised correlational method to the task of defining the nature and task of practical theology. Tracy's revised correlational method is not new to the precincts of practical theology, for it is in practical theology that the church has its most direct interaction with the secular world. Clearly, an early version of this theological method can be found in the practical theologies of Daniel Day Williams and Seward Hiltner.[2] Most theologically trained persons are familiar with Paul Tillich's theological method which correlates questions arising from our existence as humans with answers that come forth from Christian revelation. Tracy's revised correlational method is less one-sided and more reciprocal; he believes in critically correlating both questions and answers that come from various secular or non-Christian interpretations of existence with various interpretations of the questions and answers conveyed in Christian revelation (what Tracy calls "the Christian fact"). Tracy wants what he calls a "public theology"—one that can take its place in an honest, open, and mutually critical dialogue within the context of a pluralistic society. Practical theology, Tracy believes, has primarily to do with the criteria or norms for the transformation of human brokenness. Tracy wants practical theology to be fully public and able to enter into a mutually critical dialogue (or correlation) with other secular and religious criteria of transformation to be found in the richly pluralistic world in which we find ourselves today.

Tracy places his comments about practical theology within the context of a discussion of the other two great branches of theology—fundamental or philosophical theology and systematic theology. Practical theology is the most concrete, but it contains in embryonic form the theoretical structures that fundamental and systematic theology unearth through philosophical and hermeneutic reflection. All three disciplines—fundamental, systematic, and practical—are abstractions from the actual lived experience of embodied praxis. Nonetheless, fundamental theology uncovers some of the critical and abstract features of the theological task in general and the nature of practical theology in particular. Or, to put it bluntly, Tracy is saying we will never have an adequate practical theology unless we first learn to reflect critically and think abstractly about the general features of the theological task. In a word, Tracy would scoff at the simplistic suggestions that equate practical theology with uncritical immersion in the flux of immediate experience.

Thomas Ogletree develops his proposals around the idea, forcefully stated, that all theology is basically practical theology. By this he means that all theology evolves out of practical involvements with the world, has practical aims, and attempts to deal in thought and action with the basic issues of human existence. Nonetheless, in order to gain a better grasp of our experience and direct it toward these practical ends, we are forced to "distance" ourselves from our engagements and pursue "objective" studies such as exegesis, hermeneutics, philosophical and systematic theology. But the purpose of these objective studies, Ogletree argues, is still practical. Ogletree isolates three dimensions of practical theology: the meaning dimension (systematic theology), the action dimension (theological ethics), and the self dimension (pastoral care, religious education, clinical training). These arc all abstractions or objectifications from the full richness of the unity of prereflective experience. *Knowing, doing,* and *being* are all part of the original unit of experience, discovered through phenomenological description of this experience, but necessarily broken apart when we start thinking about them. Theological thought is necessary, but we must remember the practical ends toward which it is originally aimed. Finally, in spite of Ogletree's critical and philosophical concerns, he seems far less interested in moving beyond the clerical paradigm than Farley and Tracy and sees practical theology addressing the needs primarily of ministerial education.

Dennis McCann's chapter, entitled "Practical Theology and Social Action," is the first of the essays dedicated to the study of specific regions of practical theology. It begins as a personal statement about his involvement in and subsequent disillusionment with a variety of social causes prominent during the 1960s. It concludes with a telling evaluation of liberation theology and the tendency of Gustavo Gutierrez and Juan Segundo to let Marxist theories of praxis dominate and exhaust Christian understandings of love and justice. In addition, the essay is about the importance of theological ethics as a genre of practical theology and the necessity of having "middle axioms" to mediate between high-level principles such as "identification with the poor" and various concrete programs in social action such as revolutionary action or development. His chapter emphasizes a point made by several authors: that theological ethics may be the paradigmatic practical theology and is destined to play in our time a vital role in renewing the other regions of practical theology.

In "Toward a Theology of Rhetoric/Preaching," Leander Keck docs not address the wider issues of practical theology, but his essay, nonetheless, presents an interesting challenge to the call for a critical practical theology found in several of the other chapters. Keck uncovers the rhetorical dimensions of Paul's understanding of preaching the gospel. Preaching is not, for Paul, a matter of critical explanation and defense of the gospel. It is a matter of recreating the event of God's rectifying forgiveness. Preaching works through faith to change our relation to God and to set us upon a pilgrimage toward a more profound moral seriousness. Keck's essay raises the question of whether a critical and reflective practical theology can ever return once again to the immediacy of the rectifying event proclaimed and recreated in the act of preaching. Keck's view of preaching indirectly challenges all of the other chapters that call for a critical moment in practical theology.

James Fowler's chapter on "Practical Theology and the Shaping of Christian Lives" is similar to Farley's in wanting to anchor practical theology on critical reflection on "the praxis of the Christian community's life and work in its various dimensions." In light of this emphasis upon the praxis of the Christian community, Fowler defines Christian education as *Bildung* (formation) and understands it to include the "variety of informal ways, beyond instruction and catechesis, in which ecclesial communities intentionally sponsor the awakening and formation of persons in faith." A practical theology of Christian education, we can presume, would be critical reflection on the church's formation of persons. Fowler, as does Lapsley, addresses the question of whether theological ethics has a privileged role in formulating the goals of human fulfillment guiding Christian education. His answer is positive, but he shies away from an ethic of principle in favor of an ethic of disposition. This is a distinction between two approaches to ethics that I will discuss below.

Next comes James Lapsley's chapter, "Practical Theology and Pastoral Care." Much of his essay is spent addressing the issue of the relation of pastoral theology to theological ethics. Lapsley sees pastoral theology as a genre of practical theology that studies relationships within the church of tender and solicitous care for individuals and small groups. Pastoral theology unabashedly focuses on the good of the individual and will inevitably at times conflict with the good of the larger community. Pastoral theology, Lapsley argues, is only indirectly related to theological ethics; it primarily aims at discerning the next most relevant "possibility" for growth available to a suffering or broken person. Theological ethics, on the other hand, concentrates on discovering the proper norms and standards that should govern behavior in its optimal moral expressions. But finally, Lapsley does indeed point out that the pastor cannot discern relevant possibilities for a troubled person without reference to some understanding of norms. He writes that pastoral theologians need to keep in mind that their "pastoral care is always carried out with reference to some kind of norm of human conduct."

On the other hand, my chapter on "Pastoral Theology in a Pluralistic Age" explicitly argues for a prominent role for theological ethics in a practical theology of pastoral care. In fact, it contends that pastoral theology must acknowledge the pluralistic age in which we live and strive to be critical (philosophical and reflective) and public (much in the way David Tracy uses the word "public"). It is my hope that some day pastoral theology can be informed both by a critical theological ethic that will help us establish the norms of human life and dynamic psychology that will, much as Lapsley suggests, help us discern the relevant possibilities for a particular person. This blend of moral theology (theological ethics) and dynamic psychology is probably closer to Lapsley's position than one might first think. The emphasis upon the significant role for theological ethics in pastoral theology is continuous with several other chapters that affirm its central place in any reconstruction of the task of practical theology and its various regions.

Common Issues for a New Agenda

This brief overview is designed to give readers some guide to the major thrust of each chapter. But the more important goal of this introduction is to isolate the common issues that seem to surface time and again in these chapters, clarify the different positions taken, and point to the major directions the chapters collectively appear to be going. Only then can we begin to discern the distinctive outlines of some novel approaches to practical theology represented by the discussions collected in this volume. These are doubtless the issues that will need to be further addressed if progress in practical theology is actually to be achieved.

Beyond the Clerical Paradigm

Edward Farley is the first of our authors to call for practical theology to go beyond the "clerical paradigm." By this he has in mind the post-Schleiermacher tendency to associate practical theology with the specific arts of homiletics, liturgics, catechetics, and poimenics (pastoral care) needed by the ordained minister to maintain the internal life of the church. One finds such schemes in the works on practical theology by J. J. Oosterzee, F. B. Köster, W. G. T. Shedd, James M. Hoppin, and many others.[3] Farley's emphasis upon centering practical theology on a phenomenology of "ecclesial presence" is designed to shift away from exclusive concentration upon the internal life of the church and accentuate more the life of the church in the world. This shift was first called for in recent times, to my knowledge, in an insightful article by Alastair Campbell entitled "Is Practical Theology Possible?"[4] Fowler comes closest to striking the same note when he writes that practical theology gains its energy and impetus from "ecclesial passion," which should not, he quickly adds, be equated with "clerical passion." Something like this desire to go beyond the clerical paradigm is implicit in the concern for a "public" practical theology championed by Tracy, McCann, and myself. But, as I show below, the final meaning of the concern of these authors is slightly different than that of Farley.

The exceptions to this widely shared value are James Lapsley and possibly Leander Keck. It is clear that for Lapsley a practical theology of pastoral care would deal predominantly, and maybe exclusively, with what pastors do to care for people inside the church. And Keck's understanding of preaching seems to have little place for apologetics and primarily seems aimed at deepening the faith of those who already believe to some extent. It would be especially the concern of Lapsley to challenge those anxious to go beyond the "clerical paradigm" to say more about just how the needs of professional ministerial education would be accounted for in their model.

Practical Theology as Critical

The desire to go beyond the clerical paradigm takes a slightly different form in Tracy, McCann, and myself than is the case, for example, with Farley and Fowler. All five of these authors, and Ogletree as well, want theology in general and practical theology in particular to be a critical discipline. By this they mean a discipline that is reflective, that thinks about and tests in some way the affirmations of faith, that wrestles with biblical and historical criticism, that inquires into what it means to interpret a text, and that asks about the relation of faith to the various forms of secular knowledge. But Tracy, McCann, and I all emphasize even more the need for practical theology to enter a revised correlational dialogue with the other religious and secular "faiths" that make up our pluralistic society. They want the practical theologian to enter an open and honest conversation with the secular educator, the secular mental health worker, the Marxist revolutionary, the local Jewish mayor, the feminist member of the municipal council, and the fundamentalist senator with his huge popular following. This concern with pluralism is neither a capitulation to it nor romanticization of it. It is more a matter of accepting it as a given of most modern societies and learning how to respectfully deal with differences without relinquishing the Christian's convictions and his or her final obligation to help shape the common community life.

The revised correlational method in practical theology that the three of us propose goes beyond the simple desire to center practical theology on the church's presence in the world. It wants this presence to both start in faith yet end in a mutually critical dialogue between Christianity and other perspectives toward the end of shaping a common life. In all three cases, we posit a crucial role for theological ethics and moral philosophy as disciplines and tools that will help clarify issues and make choices with regard to norms and means of social and individual transformation.

An Ethics of Principle Versus an Ethics of Disposition

An interest in the role of theological ethics, either positive or negative, is not to be found in all the chapters. For instance, in Burkhart's more constructive remarks he singles out hermeneutics as the center to practical theology, whereas Farley and Ogletree speak mostly about a phenomenology of ecclesial or Christian existence as the center. Tracy, for example, would agree with the priority of interpretation for any theological enterprise, including practical theology. Our first task, for him, is to interpret the classic texts, symbols, rituals, and practices of the Christian faith. But there is a moment within practical theology (and it is just a moment, not the entire task) when the norms of transformation need to be examined by a critical theological ethic. This is much the same thing that McCann has in mind when he writes that in his middle-axiom approach the "relationship between practical theology and social action always proceeds through the discipline of social ethics." And this is much of what I have in mind when I write in my chapter, "Pastoral theology should understand itself as an expression of theological ethics, primarily concerned with the religio-ethical norms governing the human life cycle." If practical theology has to do with critical reflection on social and individual transformation, it would seem that there would need to be a place within it for a critical discipline that deals with the *norms* of social and individual existence.

But each of the proposals by Tracy, McCann, and myself seems to suggest that practical theology needs the service of an ethic of principle. An ethic of principle can most easily be defined by contrasting it with an ethic of disposition. Those committed to an ethic of disposition are primarily interested in questions such as "Who is the good person?" or "What is right virtue?" or "What is good character?" There are those, and Aristotle is alleged to have been one of them, who define the ethical task primarily in terms of answering these questions about virtue, character, and the good person. Tracy, McCann, and I seem not so much opposed to an ethic of disposition as we are interested in both supplementing it by and possibly anchoring it on an ethic of principle. An ethic of principle (often referred to as deontic ethical judgments in contrast to aretaic or dispositional ethical judgments) tries to answer what is right as an objective judgment independent of the virtue or character of the people involved.[5] The persons arguing for an ethics of principle generally do not deny the need for a dispositional ethic or the need for good people with virtue and character; rather, they would argue that we cannot have such a dispositional ethic or know who the good person is unless we first know the principles required for making such a judgment. Certainly this is the point that Tracy is making when he says that without ethical reflection—by which he means "critical theoretical reflection upon moral praxis"— practical theology can easily "be left with a purely dispositional ethics. . . ."

This contrast between those two approaches to ethics illuminates the points made by both Lapsley and Fowler with reference to my chapter. Lapsley, in trying to downplay the role of ethics in pastoral care, is primarily criticizing an ethic of principle. On the other hand, when he admits that every effort to discern possibilities for people (his understanding of the dominant focus of pastoral theology) also assumes some normative vision of human fulfillment, he is primarily articulating the crucial role of a dispositional ethic in pastoral care. I would agree with the importance of a dispositional ethic for pastoral care; this is what I mean by an ethic "of the human life cycle." The difference between us is this: I would say that an ethic of disposition is finally dependent upon an ethic of principle. A similar set of issues exists between Fowler and myself.

Theory and Practice

Both Farley and Burkhart believe that Schleiermacher had much to do with creating the split between theory and practice in practical theology. In an effort to heal this, a significant number of our authors affirm both the temporal and logical priority of practice over theory. Farley, Tracy, Ogletree, Lapsley, and Fowler all explicitly, in one fashion or another, make this affirmation in their chapters. But Tracy and Ogletree probably say the most about the theory-practice relation. The issue of their relation becomes complicated if we grant Tracy's point that practice is always "theory-laden." The difference between practice and praxis is that in the latter the theory has been made self-conscious and reflected upon critically.

The theory that is implicit in all practice is made explicit through "critical reflection" (Tracy) and "distancing" or "objectification" (Ogletree). It is precisely the task of theology to make explicit the theory implicit in the Christian life so that this life can be more self-consciously directed and appraised. Although both Tracy and Ogletree see the necessity of the theoretical turn in doing practical theology, it is clear that Tracy sees the theoretical as far more important and far more complicated than does Ogletree. It involves the highly philosophical turns of fundamental theology and the hermeneutical turns of systematic theology. In addition, the turns are not only designed to clarify the theory implicit in praxis for the faithful but to give reasons and to some extent justify this praxis to the unbelievers in our secular and pluralistic society. Furthermore, even though praxis for Tracy is prior to theory, once the reflective process has begun and we are indeed in the theoretical moment, the more abstract features of theory are more determinative than the less abstract and more concrete features. This is why for Tracy even a practical theology that was truly reflective about its theoretical base would sooner or later, if honest and rigorous, have to back up and consider some of the remotest of metaphysical principles. Ogletree, on the other hand, although building a place for theory as a distancing moment within the life of praxis, seems primarily interested in theory for what it can do to teach the faithful and less interested in a revised correlational dialogue with other praxis models in our pluralistic situation.

The Role of the Social Sciences

In recent years, especially in the United States, practical theology has had an especially close relation to the social sciences. Theological ethics has had a close relation to sociology, economics, and political science. Pastoral care has had a close relation to psychotherapeutic psychology, personality theory, and developmental psychology. Religious education has had a close relation to learning theory, developmental psychology, and more recently social and cultural anthropology. Other similar examples can be cited for liturgics and homiletics. Sometimes the relation to the social sciences is so prominent in a particular region of practical theology that the region comes close to being identified with that science, such as has been the case in pastoral care's identification with psychotherapy.

Several of the chapters discuss the proper role of the social sciences in practical theology, especially those by Tracy, Ogletree, Fowler, Lapsley, and myself. On the whole, there is a considerable amount of agreement about the role of the social sciences. Ogletree, I believe, makes a representative statement when he argues that the primary task of these sciences is to "surface dynamics that constrain and channel our action possibilities." The social sciences do not dictate norms, it seems, and only indirectly make suggestions for appropriate strategies and skills. Only when theological ethics tells us what our goals in action *should be* can the social sciences meaningfully tell us about what constrains and channels our actions toward reaching these goals. *In fact, one way to talk about the task of practical theology is to say it has the job of both stating our ultimate goals and then expressing them in more proximate terms* (along with the appropriate means of attaining them) *in light of the social, cultural, and psychological factors that constrain and channel the action possibilities of the people involved.*

However, all of these discussions of the role of the social sciences could have gone further, at least in some respects. There may be a more positive, yet still limited, role for the social sciences in helping to establish the properly normative interests of practical theology. Some of the social sciences—especially personality theory, developmental psychology, and sociobiology—contain empirical information about the central tendencies and central needs of human beings. This kind of information, as I have argued elsewhere, may make important contributions to our normative judgments, especially in situations where humans are disputing about what their real needs are.[6] Knowledge of our central tendencies and needs never dictates our norms of action. But such knowledge is generally relevant; at least from one important moral point of view, what we consider morally right, and therefore normative, is that which justly and impartially actualizes the widest range possible of compatible central human tendencies and needs.[7]

But finally, only Tracy points out the need to use the social sciences with an eye toward criticizing them as well. Not only can the social sciences uncover the ideologies and neuroses that constrain and channel our social and individual action, but in turn, the social sciences themselves often contain normative horizons that are distorted and need criticism. This is one of the functions, Tracy would contend, of the mutually critical correlation that should occur between practical theology and any social science that pretends to throw light on praxis.

A Critique of Liberation Theology

The comments about liberation theology are not extensive in these chapters, but the ones put forth are indeed noteworthy. We already have reviewed McCann's analysis which claims that at least in some liberation theologians, mainly Segundo and Gutierrez, there occurs a politicization of the gospel. This occurs, he claims, because Marxist interpretations of praxis, with its sanctions for violent revolution, constitute the controlling framework in these theologies by which the mandate to identify with the poor is interpreted. In addition, Tracy implicitly criticizes liberation theology for elevating praxis to the point of negating theory. And Farley implicitly criticizes liberation theology for emphasizing the social-political aspects of praxis at the exclusion of the personal-existential and the ecclesiastical. His understanding of practical theology would affirm yet organize all three—the social-political, the personal-existential, and the ecclesiastical—under the umbrella of ecclesial presence transforming the world.

Proposals for Future Directions

The future, to my mind, rests in successfully amplifying and differentiating two important features of any complete practical theology: (1) a hermeneutics of the moral praxis of the Christian community, and (2) what is meant by thinking critically about it. In other publications[8] I have isolated five dimensions of practical thought and action that can be used for both interpretative and critical purposes.

In interpreting the moral praxis of any community, including the Christian community, we should be concerned to understand five interrelated levels of practical thought and action. These five levels are: (1) a metaphorical level, (2) an obligational level, (3) a tendency-need level, (4) a contextual level, and (5) a rule, role, communicational level. To understand the first level (the highest level) of moral praxis we should ask, what are the dominant metaphors used by a community to symbolize its apprehension of the ultimate context of experience and how do these metaphors influence the lower levels of practical thought? Second, we should ask, what are the dominant and most general principles of obligation functioning in the community? Third, what are the human tendencies and needs that the community addresses and how do the higher-level metaphors of ultimacy and principles of obligation relate to these needs? Fourth, what are the major cultural, social, and psychological forces conditioning the practical action? And fifth, what then are the concrete actions, rules, roles, and patterns of communication that flow forth from judgments at these higher levels?

These levels can be used to interpret the practical life of a particular congregation and, in addition, can be used to analyze the strength and weakness of various disciplines (such as systematic theology, anthropology, sociology, psychology, organizational development) that one might want to apply to the study of the practical life of a congregation.[9] But the same five levels can be used also to guide critical evaluation and reflection. However, the logical interrelation of these levels for critical and constructive practical theological purposes is too complex to elaborate in this introduction; it is a question I have addressed in several recent publications.[10] In the future, we doubtless will see a host of proposals emerging as the church tries to renew theological reflection at the level of its practical life in the world.

It is now time to let these nine chapters speak for themselves. I commend these chapters to the reader and hope that, in addition to whatever immediate illumination they afford, they also help set an agenda for the renewal of theology in all its practical forms.

NOTES

1. David Tracy, *Blessed Rage for Order: The New Pluralism in Theology* (New York: Seabury, 1975); *The Analogical Imagination* (New York: Seabury, Crossroad Books, 1981).
2. Daniel Day Williams, "Truth in a Theological Perspective," *Journal of Religion* (October 1948), and *The Minister and the Care of Souls* (New York: Harper and Brothers, 1961); Seward Hiltner, *Preface to Pastoral Theology* (New York: Abingdon, 1958).
3. Hiltner, *Preface to Pastoral Theology,* pp. 47, 48.

4. Alastair Campbell, "Is Practical Theology Possible?" *Scottish Journal of Theology* (May 1972).
5. William Frankena, *Ethics* (Englewood Cliffs, NJ: Prentice-Hall, 1973), p. 9.
6. I have amplified this point in several forthcoming publications, "The Estrangement of Pastoral Care from Ethics," *Concilium;* "Psychology as Religio-Ethical Thinking," *Journal of Religion; Religious Ethics and Pastoral Care* (Philadelphia: Fortress).
7. This view of the relation of moral obligation to our central human tendencies and needs is well expressed in Peter Singer, *The Expanding Circle: Ethics and Sociobiology* (New York: Farrar, Straus, & Giroux, 1981). Other excellent books that point in this direction are Mary Midgley, *Beast and Man* (New York: Cornell University Press, 1978) and George Pugh, *The Biological Origins of Human Values* (New York: Basic Books, 1977).
8. See especially my integrating essay in *Building Effective Ministry* (Harper & Row, forthcoming).
9. I give examples of how this can be done in *Building Effective Ministry.*
10. These forthcoming publications are principally the ones listed in note 6.

I

HISTORICAL
PERSPECTIVES

Genre q theology - narrowed

1 Wisdom - It is knowledge q God
2. science - discipline q inquiry
                      and study

3 Sciences - generic term for a cluster
          q independent studies

4. Systematic Theology
          discrete field q inquiry

p. 30
Very structure q theological studies
alienates the whole enterprise
from praxis.

2. Theology and Practice Outside the Clerical Paradigm

EDWARD FARLEY

THE expression "theology and practice" suggests both the general issue of the praxis dimensions, contents, and references of theology as well as issues that attend one of the traditional subdisciplines of theological study, practical theology. The general issue is as old as theology itself but has a special thematization in the debate fostered by the Aristotelian vision of the sciences about whether theology is a practical science. The most recent form of this debate is now occurring under the question of theology's relation to praxis as the situationality of corrupt corporate and political life. Practical theology too has a long history, but its status as an unwelcome and embarrassing adopted child in some schools and as the queen of the theological sciences in others suggests that all is not quiet on that front. This chapter is largely preoccupied with refining and articulating the problem of theology and practice. Three general theses preside over the attempt:

1. The two issues, the relation of theology and practice and the question of practical theology, both reflect a common historical legacy that is in part responsible for their problematic status and that calls for a single solution.
2. The problem that attends both clusters of issues cannot be formulated as long as the question of the *genre* of theology itself is omitted.
3. The problem of theology and practice is very much the result of a historical legacy that accordingly, needs to be uncovered, sorted out, and subjected to thoroughgoing analysis and criticism.

This essay will proceed then in a five-step argument. The first step attempts to formulate the problem of the genre of theology, yielding, I hope, the essential ambiguity of the term "theology." The second step identifies the loss of one of the meanings of theology as a genre and argues that this loss had fateful consequences for theology and practice. The third step describes the present alienation of theology and practice. The fourth step takes up the problem of practical theology. The fifth step offers some modest suggestions for addressing the problem.

The Problem of the Genre of Theology

Theology is, we are told, a discipline, a course of studies, a career and teaching specialty, a necessity for ministry, a Hellenistic-Christian mode of thinking that no self-respecting Buddhist, Hindu, or Jew would dream of imitating. It is churchly, Christological, biblical, ratiocinative, situational, chauvinistic, legitimating, critical, objectivist, personal, academic, concrete, and, of course, practical. The problem is that many if not most of these missiles have been launched at a different target. Two types or levels of ambiguity are at work here. One is the consequence of failing to designate the situation or context in which the word is working. Hence, it works one way when the assumed context is a school for the training of clergy and another when the context is simply human beings or the community of faith. I mention this ambiguity of context not to pursue it but because I do not want simply to assume that the seminary is the only possible context for posing the question of theology and practice. The other ambiguity is the ambiguity of genre, on which we are now focusing.

The ambiguity of genre calls attention to the *sort of thing* theology is. In an obvious oversimplification I would distinguish four different meanings of theology as a genre. As a term, theology was, as we all know, appropriated from Hellenic philosophy by early Christianity, and its initial use did not vary significantly from Plato and Aristotle. In the first distinctively Christian usage the term simply meant the knowledge of God. And this is the original genre. Theology is an *episteme,* a *scientia,* an act or cognitive disposition in which the self-disclosing God is grasped as disclosed. In this sense theology is simply what Christian faith is all about, for knowledge of God in this sense and salvation coincide. This meaning of theology has, of course, a long history,[1] but throughout that history theology never means simply an abstract, impersonal knowledge. It *is* knowledge of God. The seventeenth century seems to be the last period to use the term in this way. In that literature God was the one, true, archetypal theologian, because only God had true, archetypal self-knowledge. That literature followed the Middle Ages in calling theology a *habitus,* a disposition, power, act of the soul itself. And some of the writers argued that the kind of disposition or habit it was was *wisdom.*[2] The genre of theology is, therefore, an existential, personal act and relation of the human self—namely wisdom.

The Greek term, *episteme,* and the Latin translation, *scientia,* are themselves ambiguous in genre. They mean knowledge, the *habitus,* but they can also mean science, discipline; and *episteme* did mean that in Aristotle's classification of sciences in the *Metaphysics.* With the rise of schools in Christendom, especially after the Carolingian renaissance, and especially with the origin of the universities in Europe, theology came also to refer to another sort of thing, another genre, namely a discipline of inquiry and study.[3] We should not be too quick to think we know what this genre is. We are, to be sure, used to thinking under the divisions of sciences, disciplines, fields. However, we are not used to thinking of theology as a science or discipline. There is, of course, a set of courses and designated faculty called systematic theology within a larger faculty of studies, but this genre we are talking about is not a subdiscipline. It is simply the one, single science, parallel to philosophy, rhetoric, and astronomy, with its own object and proper method.

Both of these genres of theology disappeared long ago. To recall them we shall simply designate the first theology/*habitus* and the second theology/science. The third genre of theology did not arise and could not arise until something happened to the second genre, to theology as a science. The story is a familiar one. It happened as the result of that vast Copernican revolution of religious faith, institutionality, and intellection which began in the Renaissance and Reformation and ended in the pervasive criticisms of both faith and theology that we associate with the Enlightenment. This watershed of change obtained institutionalization in the new, modern universities of Europe such as Halle and Göttingen, and when it was over, one thing was firmly entrenched in the interpretation of religion—the critical principle.[4] And with that, theology the *habitus* and theology the one science were replaced by theological *sciences*. The new institution is the theological faculty: chairs of Old Testament, New Testament, dogmatics, and church history. With this development, the term theology obtains a different genre. It becomes a generic term for a cluster of relatively independent studies; it becomes a term like law, medicine, or liberal arts. Once theological sciences developed, a new problem appeared—how to relate them to each other in unity and coherence. And with that problem came a new literature, called by German theologians who were its first authors theological encyclopedia.

We have already mentioned the fourth genre. In the modern faculty of theology a shadow of the old dogmatics remains in the form of systematic (or constructive, or philosophical) theology. The term "theology" sometimes refers to this discrete field of inquiry, study, and thinking.

Have all these genres survived into the present? It is clear that they have not survived as genres of theology, but there are modern versions of them. Contemporary theology and religion are not indifferent to postures, cognitive dispositions appropriate to faith. Modernity does not call this theology but theological understanding. Of late this has been narrowed to something yielded by hermeneutics, occurring in the interpretation of texts. Theology/*habitus* survives not as theology, but as insight, existential knowledge, understanding.[5] Theology as science is here not as a single undertaking, but as various scholarly disciplines. Theology/faculty is with us, even terminologically, when we speak of theological schools. It is, however, a rapidly fading usage, being replaced by the term "seminary" in professional schools and "Religious Studies" in the colleges and universities. Theology as a subdiscipline, systematic theology, remains as *the* modern usage and symptomizes the narrowed conception of theology.

Sketchy as this account is, these sortings enable us to see why little clarity comes forth about theology and practice when the genre itself is undesignated. Obviously, theology/*habitus* has a different relation to praxis than theology/faculty and theology/science.

The Loss of Theology/*Habitus* and Its Consequences

We move now to the second step, the tracing of the consequences of the modern narrowing of theology. Theology/*habitus* and theology/science more or less coincided from the Middle Ages through the seventeenth century, and this coincidence constituted a fundamental equivocation in the genre of theology. Both usages disappeared under the impact of the Enlightenment and the rise of the modern university. We shall not attempt a historical account of that disappearance. It has to do with criticisms of the traditional fundamental and natural theologies, the critical principle and historical sense, and changing paradigms of authority. Suffice it to say that once the term theology named a faculty of studies, it was no longer thought of as either a personal-existential *habitus* or wisdom or as a single science. This left theological faculties with a severe problem. The discrete fields were, without question, scholarly undertakings, but what is the theological faculty itself and why has it any place in the university at all?

It was Schleiermacher who offered the solution to this problem, which is why his *Brief Outline of the Study of Theology* is a seminal work. According to Schleiermacher the theological sciences are not divisions of a region of being or knowledge but, like the medical and legal sciences, ordered toward a professional goal. Their unity in other words is teleological and practical. Like physicians and lawyers, ministers play an important leadership role in society and the education of ministers has as legitimate a place in the university as the education of lawyers and physicians. In this solution there is no theology/*habitus* and no theology as a single science. There are discrete academic fields of teaching and research that are unified generally by their contribution to the training of the clerical leadership of the church and more specifically by their relation to the essence of Christianity. This work of Schleiermacher's was neither the first work of its kind nor was it highly influential as a plan for theological studies. And yet it is indicative of the contributions of the nineteenth-century works of this sort in that it proposes a way of conceiving theological study that justifies its presence in a modern university, retains the independence of fields of scholarship, and founds it in the church and the ministry. That is Schleiermacher's contribution. At the same time this solution had two far-reaching consequences for the relation of theology and practice.

The first is what we might call the parochialization or even the clericalization of theology. Schleiermacher's anti-Enlightenment program to salvage "theology" by founding it both in a universal fundamental ontology of human being and in the determinacy of a corporate historical faith is well known. However, the solution of the *Brief Outline* does not propose simply a correlation between theology and a determinate historical faith but a correlation between theology and the *clergy* of that faith carrying out their leadership tasks. This is the fundamental reason why theology, namely theology/faculty, is practical. It pertains to the leadership praxis of the clergy as it, under the sponsorship of the State, serves the church.[6] And, likewise, this is the clue to the nature of practical theology as a field of study. Practical theology inquires into the right procedures to be followed by the church's leadership in its attempt to promote the health of the community of faith. The concern here is not so much with the technology of the tasks but with the rules under which the tasks occur. The eighteenth-century pietist theologians before Schleiermacher had already talked about practical theology as applied theology, but they had not quite resolved the question whether the application was to the moral life or to clerical tasks. Schleiermacher resolves the issue. Applied theology means application to clerical responsibilities and tasks.

All of us will recognize this solution and language. It is the world we live in. That is, we are accustomed to thinking of theology as theology/faculty, the cluster of studies pertinent to the training of clergy. And we are accustomed to posing the issue of practicality as the issue of funding clerical tasks and responsiblities. This way of relating theology and practice comes to us from Schleiermacher and the nineteenth-century theological encyclopedias, the pietist and German solution to the problem of justifying theology/faculty's presence in the university. It was not a solution for American universities. As we know, the eventual

American institution for clerical education was, with a few exceptions, not the university but the seminary. In the course of the
nineteenth century the American seminaries imitated the plan of
study of the German universities and as college departments of
religion grew, they, at least until recently, imitated the seminaries. We can see already how this created problems of relating
theology and practice, since both theology and practice are correlated with *clergy* education. Ingenious as the solution was, it
created enormous problems of conceiving how theology has anything to do with institutions, human beings, or culture outside
the leadership of the church. In other words if theology is related
to practice simply by way of clerical leadership, it does not have
an essential praxis element related to world as such. "Theology"
in other words does not refer to the self-understanding of the
community of faith as it exists in relation to the *world*.

The second consequence of Schleiermacher's solution is a way
of relating theory and practice, and this too is our legacy and the
air we continue to breathe. We realize what a monumental alter-
ation Schleiermacher's solution represented when we consider
what it replaced. Theology as a *habitus* is, we recall, a cognitive-
ly, insightfully disposed posture that attends salvation, a knowledge of the self-disclosing God. As such it is for the sake of God,
but that means for God's appointed salvific end of the human
being. Theology in this sense cannot be anything but practical.
Theologia practica is simply the *habitus* viewed as to its end. In
the sixteenth and seventeenth centuries there were sporadic attempts to distinguish within theology aspects that were "thetic,"
having to do with confession, affirmation, and belief, and aspects
that were practical, having to do with moral and ascetic life and
also matters of the church. This distinction was not yet an identification of fields of study or disciplines, but it did support a way
of distinguishing theory and practice. Theory meant that aspect
of the *habitus*, or wisdom, in which the divine object evokes acknowledgment, belief. Practice meant that aspect of the *habitus*,
or wisdom, in which the divine object sets requirements of obedience and life. Both reside in the single existential *habitus* called
theology. Theory/practice is based here on what could be called
a phenomenology of theology as a *habitus*.

With Schleiermacher's solution and the clericalization of theology comes another view of theory and practice. Theology as a faculty of sciences is unified by church leadership as its telos. Practical theology as one part of the faculty concerns the rules for the application of criteria obtained from historical studies to tasks of church leadership. The language of theory and practice pervades the literature on the structure of theological study from before Schleiermacher throughout the nineteenth century. In that literature Bible, church history, dogmatics, and ethics fall on the theory side; practical theology on the practice side. And this too is a world we recognize immediately. At the root of this way of distinguishing the two is not a phenomenology of a *habitus* but a phenomenology of the educational requirements for clergy responsibilities. The clergy need to know the teachings and history of the church (the theory) in order to have a theory of ministerial practice. What happens to the *habitus* in this approach? That is, what happens to the existential-personal posture that grasps the transforming realities of faith?

As far as the structure of theological study goes, it disappears into the realm of the personal, of opinion, taste, autobiography, a realm that theological education is not concerned with as education, only as part of the desired formative environment of education. And all modern theological education seems to be built on this chasm, this dualism between the cognitive-personal element, now exported from education and study, and the cognitive element required by clerical leadership and provided by independent scholarly undertakings. In sum theory and practice are related in this post-Schleiermacher solution as academic and applied aspects of the training for clergy.

This analysis of the consequences of the loss of theology/*habitus* poses for us three issues:

1. Is "theology" coincident with or reducible to a group term for a faculty of studies?
2. Is the relation of theology and practice simply a feature of clergy education?
3. Are theory and practice terms for relating academic and applied aspects of a clergy-oriented course of studies to each other?

The Alienation of Theology and Practice

We move now to a more direct formulation of the problem of theology and practice. There is a certain irony in the American preoccupation with theology and practice given the perennial attempts to rehabilitate theology and theological education. The concern for practice occurs on at least three levels and has generated three different agenda. The first reflects the loss of theology as a *habitus*. Expressing a category or genre confusion, it presupposes that theology is a faculty of independent scholarly undertakings and then tries to uncover the personal-existential relevance of these undertakings. One characteristic solution uncovered in recent years by both churches and theological schools is the therapeutic, which masquerades as a pseudo-theological *habitus*. Another characteristic concern is the attempt to restore this existential-personal dimension by extracurricular programs of formation. The second agenda reflects Schleiermacher's solution to the unity of theological studies but transforms that away from his focus on theologically derived rules for ministerial practice to a technology of practice. Its question is, how can theology meet the professional needs of clergy carrying out their task in the actual church in the actual world? When the theological school is the context of this rehabilitation, the theology in question is theology/faculty, and the question means, how can the various enterprises of study (study of Irenaean theodicies, resurrection narratives, Gadamerian hermeneutics, the exegesis of 1 Thessalonians) be useful for the tasks of church leadership?

Attempts to rehabilitate theology along personalist and professional lines are centuries old. The third attempt may reflect a new paradigm. It senses that certain dimensions of ecclesiality may be resources for the critique and interpretation of global and local social crises, especially those rooted in enduring structures of oppression. If theology/faculty is being addressed, the question turns out to mean, how can the existing fields of the theological school contribute to radical cultural criticism and speak to the present situation? If theology as the subdiscipline (systematic theology) is being addressed, it means, how can this subdiscipline be so transformed as to do situational theology? In both cases the conventional structure of theological study is pre-supposed and the genre of theology is not designated. In the first case the criticism addresses the established fiefdoms that orga-nize theological curricula and issues an invitation to curricular combat. In the second case the question is addressed to a subdis-cipline but not to other areas of theological study.

We can see now why theological education, in spite of decades of practice-oriented self-renewal, interprets itself and is experi-enced by students as alienated from praxis. And we can see why it is that the more it rehabilitates itself by extending theology as applied, the deeper the alienation becomes. The reason is that, given the theory/practice structure of theological education, that cluster of studies called practical theology is many steps removed from whatever unifying understanding is generated by faith it-self; and all the elements of faith, corporate and individual, that do have potentially explosive praxis dimensions are relegated to the unapplied, theoretical, academic side of the plan of study.

All three of these agenda of rehabilitation express valid con-cerns, but they tend to be easily trivialized because the *theology* they would transform is either undesignated, or it means the to-tality of independent, scholarly undertakings cannot meaningful-ly entertain the qualifier "practical." The rehabilitation at-tempts, therefore, appear to be defeated from the start by the dispersion of theology into independent areas of scholarship and by the ambiguity of genre. Our thesis, in other words, is that the very structure of theological studies alienates the whole enter-prise from praxis. Hence, proposals on behalf of praxis made to that structure are quickly and easily absorbed and trivialized.

When we turn then to the theme of theology and practice, it is clear that there is no single problem but a complex cluster of problems. This is apparent both from the ambiguity of the genre of theology and from the many meanings and dimensions of practice. Three dimensions of practice are especially prominent, and they correspond to the three types of the rehabilitation of theology. They are the personal-existential, the social-political, and the ecclesiastical. Clearly, the old sense of theology/*habitus* captures the first dimension. Conceived this way, theology itself is a practice, a term for the experiential dimension, the shaping of the self, the life pilgrimage of the human being in transcendental, decisional, existential modes. The political/social dimension of practice not only pertains to the corporate, the intersubjective, the ecclesial structure of the life of faith, but to the concrete historical situation in which faith occurs. And this unavoidably is a political situation. The ecclesiastical dimension of practice pertains to the institutionality of the community of faith, including the requirements of its leadership. We have in these three dimensions of praxis Cartesian or Cartesian-Kierkegaardian, Marxist, and Schleiermacherian paradigms. To the degree that we can establish them as necessary dimensions of practice as it occurs for faith, we have a threefold criterion by which to measure ways of relating theology and practice.

The problem is, in theological education, the third or clerical paradigm has so dominated as to exclude the other two, not totally from the life of schools, but as paradigms that affect the structure of theological study. I am contending that it is this exclusion that is responsible for the failure of the rehabilitation attempts, for the reduction of the question of practice to ministerial technology. If this is the case, one task before us is to find some way of incorporating both existential and political paradigms of practice in theological education, thereby retaining but broadening the ecclesiastical paradigm.

The Problem of Practical Theology
Our fourth step moves us to the question of practical theology. The term "practical theology" occurred originally to describe theology/*habitus* or theology as a single science as having a practical end.[7] The earliest proposal that a special set of materials be read pertaining to ministerial tasks comes from the sixteenth-century theologian Hyperius, but the term "practical theology" is not used for that. The first usage of the term for a designated set of studies comes from the Dutch theologian Voetius. He includes under the name a group of studies that embrace both moral theology (ethics) and church government. From that time through the eighteenth century there was no clear-cut usage of the term for simply areas of ministerial activity. However, once the standard fourfold pattern of theological

disciplines was obtained, the pattern of Bible, church history, dogmatics, and practical theology, the latter referred to studies pertaining to ministerial activities: catechetics, preaching, pastoral care. It is frequently thought of as applied theology, but the "applied" refers to tasks of ministry, not individual or social aspects of moral life.

There is great variety in the interpretation of this area of studies throughout the nineteenth century. Again, Schleiermacher is a pivotal figure. It had become commonplace prior to Schleiermacher to distinguish practical theology from the theoretical disciplines as the applied part of the theological studies. In that scheme practical theology was a kind of appendix to those studies with little integral relation to them. By identifying the subject matter of practical theology as the *rules* for the exercise of the ministries of the church, Schleiermacher identified a subject matter for the field, and by making those rules subject to the essence of Christianity, he found a way to integrate the field into theology as a whole.[8] In this proposal practical theology, at least on paper, came close to being a discipline. But Schleiermacher's proposal was not taken up. In the literature to follow practical theology became more and more a theological technology. Its concern was for methods for preserving and extending the Christian community, the science and art of the functions of ministry.[9] But since there is no overall method or overall science of the functions, what remains are the specific tasks of preaching, teaching, pastoral care, church government, and missions. Hence, practical theology never itself became a discipline or science but like theology became a generic term embracing a number of more specific studies. Thus a single area of theological studies that mediated biblical and historical materials and the issue of the community of faith's self-perpetuation, world-oriented mission, and institutional tasks never developed. In other words practical theology never has existed and does not now exist as a discipline. The closest it came to this was as a gleam in Schleiermacher's eye.

What we have instead are specific studies, inquiries, and teaching areas pertaining to clerical tasks and responsibilities. And here the problems begin. Recall that theology/*habitus* no longer has anything to do with theological study. This means that there is no general ideal of personal-existential understanding or insight that sets the aim of such studies. Theology as a single science is replaced with various independent disciplines. There is the legacy of regarding some of these disciplines as theoretical in contrast to the applied, practical disciplines. But the original pre-Enlightenment, authority-oriented way of being subject to those disciplines, to the authority of Scripture, or to church confessions is now not operative and has not been replaced with a new paradigm. Hence, the discrete areas of study in practical theology are supposed to be subject to some larger circle of theological disciplines, but there is no paradigm making clear what that means. At the same time, as areas of study in a post-Enlightenment theological encyclopedia, each one is supposed to be a discipline, with all the accoutrements of a discipline—specialist teachers coming from specialist graduate programs. What is it that establishes these as disciplines if there is no discipline of practical theology and if they are virtually severed from the structure of theological study? The answer is, their discrete subject matter (some area of ministerial work) as it is rendered objective and scholarly by some satellite science, by rhetoric, psychology, social science, business science, and so forth. (A similar thing happens also to the other areas of study in the theological curriculum, but that is not our present concern.) This creates the typical character of the subdiscipline of the practical theology field, a combination of a functionalist temper that regards tasks and activities of ministry as the subject matter with one or more extratheological disciplines that provide the scholarly aspect.

This state of affairs has a number of consequences. As the so-called practical area, it exists in contrast to the theory area, thereby emptying itself of theory responsibility even though its subdisciplines are themselves a *theoria* of practice and not just actual practice. Practical theology itself is simply a generic term, a catalogue label. Thus, when the subdisciplines try to found themselves "theologically," the only thing they can do is build some sort of bridge from the independent disciplines of the so-called academic side: from the Old Testament to preaching, from moral theology to pastoral care, and so forth. In other words there is no gathering up of these studies, as Scheiermacher proposed in his notion of the essence of Christianity, into a clear criteriology for these fields. Finally, because of the clericalization of theology/faculty, that is, the procuring of the unity of theological matters into making pastoral leadership the end and goal, and because of the control the culture or satellite disciplines exercise on these disciplines, practical theology is increasingly vulnerable to the accusation that it is ordered toward the maintenance of middle-class religion.[10]

To the degree that the functionalist/technician paradigm governs these disciplines, it perpetuates maintenance roles of clergy in the culture and as such legitimates the structures that encapsulate social oppression. This is not to say a critical element is not exercised in these areas, but this element is the result of bringing together the task of ministry with the satellite discipline and sometimes with another area of theology. Hence, one can make critical progress in using exegesis in preaching or avoiding dogmatism in counseling. Criticism in this sense is still functioning in the sense of the first Enlightenment. And it is a further sign of the clericalization of theological study in which the world, society, oppression, the whole collective environment, finds no thematic expression in practical theology, or in fact in the structure of theological study itself.

Ecclesial Presence: The Reintegration of the Personal, the Political, and the Ecclesiastical

The various criticisms offered throughout this chapter add up to a portrayal of the problematic of theology and practice. It is time to draw them together. The one fundamental criticism is of the clerical paradigm of the unity of theology as a faculty of studies. I have argued that this paradigm is built on the loss of theology/*habitus* or theological understanding and also the loss of theology as a single science. The consequence is that theological understanding is either compartmentalized in the curriculum or placed outside of education altogether as spiritual formation. A further consequence is that theory and practice are reinterpreted as curricular divisions with sad results for both sides. Further, the clerical paradigm, limiting praxis to ministerial professional activities, excludes the social paradigm from the structure of studies and from its own version of practice, thus unwittingly perpetuating ecclesiastical institutions whatever their role in societal injustice. Practical theology as a subfield of study absorbs these problems and ends up as a set of fairly isolated studies, so controlled by their satellite sciences that they have lost access to their proper criteria. In other words, the present structure of theological study alienates theology from practice at all three levels: the personal, the societal, and the churchly.

These criticisms help us to see our task and set our agenda. The most general way of expressing that task is the overcoming of this alienation of theology and practice. The alienation pervades the religious community in all its institutions, but our concern is primarily with that alienation as it appears in the way theology as a faculty of studies is approached. Our central agenda then is the restructuring of theological study. Although clergy education in the seminary and divinity school remains the primary institution for theological study, I do not want to so formulate the problem as to make it valid only for ministerial pedagogy. The study of theology can and should occur in the churches, in the colleges and universities, by ministers no longer attending schools, in special locations in the culture. It is in fact the reduction of the question of theological study to a clergy pedagogy that has excluded it from most of these environments. However, the proposal I have in mind is not indifferent to clergy pedagogy, since it is driven by the conviction that clergy pedagogy itself needs a plan of theological study that is not unified simply by future clerical tasks and responsibilities.

Our focus on theological study is intended to clarify one of the ambiguities mentioned earlier, the ambiguity of context. We are talking about theology in *some* kind of educational situation, but we cannot resolve the ambiguity of the genre of theology. The reason is that the different usages (genres) of theology describe potentially valid dimensions of theology. This statement, however, only makes sense in the light of a broader and more formal definition of theology than we have yet offered. In the context of the history of religions, *theology* is that activity (or product of the activity) of any historical religious faith in which it attempts to ascertain its own nature, reality, and truth. In this sense there is a Jewish theology, a Buddhist theology, and so forth. In this formal definition as applied to the Christian religion, *theology* would refer to that activity (or product thereof) of the ecclesial community in which it ascertains its own nature, reality, and truth, and this would include that which is given to it, which it undergoes, attests, is receptive to. With this formal definition in mind we turn to three of the genres we considered earlier. *Theology/habitus* (i.e., theological understanding) is this ascertaining of reality and truth in the form of the persistent cognitive or insightful posture of the believer. *Theology/science* is the ascertaining of reality and truth in the form of self-conscious and rigorous inquiry under appropriate criteria and the critical principle. *Theology/faculty* is that ascertaining of reality and truth as it occurs through appropriate disciplines of a corporate educational setting. Because of my conviction that the inherited structure of study itself alienates theology and practice, the suggestions that follow will have to do with theology, that is, the organization of theological study, but not so as to ignore the other genres.

Let us first distinguish two ways in which a field of study can have a unity. First, in the *technological approach* the different parts or areas of a field are unified to the degree that they help qualify a person for a certain future function. This does not mean that technology is the subject matter of study, not that, as the eventual goal, it is the unity of studies. Obviously, this is the way any set of professional studies is unified, in that the studies function to qualify the professional as professional. We can call the second a *regional approach* because the studies are unified by the fact that they are required for the understanding of some entity, state of affairs, process, or region. These two approaches help us to see the difference between theology as faculty, unified by the requirements of understanding some region or reality, and theology as faculty unified by the requirements of the profession. The history of the last three centuries of theological education is a history of transition from a regional approach to a technological approach. The technological approach is what we are calling the clerical paradigm. As an approach to the structure and unity of theological study, it has the following problems:

1. The structure of theological study is not identical with clerical pedagogical needs.
2. While there are certain formal features about the ministry that prompt some to speak about it as a profession (for instance, it does have designated social roles and required qualifications), there is also something about it that the concept of profession does not at all capture. Since every Christian herself/himself is as such not defined by parochial responsibilities but by participation in ecclesial existence and by ends set by redemption, that definition is not suspended when that person takes on tasks of church leadership. The exercise of ministry does not abandon but intensifies the need for theological understanding (the *habitus*) which presumably characterizes the Christian as such. This means that the education for ministry cannot simply be qualification for a profession but an accumulative experience of understanding (insight) that is correlative to truths and realities presenting themselves to be understood.
3. Finally, the technological approach has fostered the various consequences, such as theory and practice divisions, on which we have already commented.

I conclude then that some form of regional approach to the unity of theological study needs to be restored. I now state this in more detail, taking up first the requirements that this calls for, and then offering a hypothesis concerning the region that can unify theological studies.

The first requirement is that theology/*habitus* or theological understanding must be restored. The alternatives to this are simply settling for an aim of theological education that is exhausted when certain professional skills are learned or settling for an aim that is simply the accumulation of information from independent areas of study. I would submit that theological understanding is the telos, the aim of any course of theological study, whenever it occurs. The second requirement is that theology/science be restored. The problem of restoring theology as a single, rigorous and reflective discipline does not mean recalling the Middle Ages but discovering how various areas of study contribute to theological understanding. This must not endanger the gains of these disciplines, especially by suppressing the critical principle by which they are disciplines. But it does mean discerning how they do contribute to the knowledge of the unifying region of study. In short it is discovering how the areas of study in a program of study are theological.

The third requirement is that a way be found to incorporate as a pervasive element in the course of studies praxis in the sense of the social and political situation. Even those schools that have a clear and maximal commitment to social praxis seem not to have found a way to do this. This is because the general question of the total structure of theological study has not been raised. The result is simplistic ways of relating theology and social/political praxis in theological study. I mean, for example, the proposals to have each course attempt to build a bridge to the situation on the assumption that there is a direct correlation between every specific aspect or level of teaching and the political context. The schools are left then with the dominant clerical paradigm and its identification of praxis with professional responsibilities with the result that the social praxis element is present atomistically and sporadically.

What follows is not a solution to all these problems but a suggestion about a possible direction to pursue. There is, it seems, a region, an inclusive reality to which theological understanding and theological science are correlated. We could of course say that God is that reality, but as soon as we say that, we have to designate how that reality is so available as to order educational undertakings. I would submit rather that ecclesiality or ecclesial existence is that region. I mean by that something partly given in history, and something ideal, normative, and eschatological. And because the sort of thing ecclesiality is as a corporate historical community is a network of redemption, we should say that the region we have in mind is ecclesiality as it perdures in history and the world. In other words, the unifying region of theological studies is ecclesial presence. To grasp ecclesial presence is to engage in a complex, historical undertaking since ecclesial presence is a certain corporate historical way in which faith occurs in the world. At the same time it is also to grasp the normative claims set by that presence, to struggle, in other words, with reality and truth. We can see, even if very dimly, how ecclesial presence might yield areas and tasks of study. But the question of this essay is whether or not ecclesial redemptive presence is a region or reality that lends itself to a thematization of praxis. I argued previously that the older approach to theological study arose from a phenomenology of theology as a *habitus* that set requirements for the study itself. While contending that the *habitus,* theological understanding, be restored as the aim, the telos, of theological study, I am now suggesting that a phenomenology of ecclesial presence may yield the divisions of study. It would be premature to attempt that phenomenology or to derive the divisions it might yield, but we should at least pursue the matter in connection with what has been called practical theology.

Practical theology under the clerical paradigm is not a discipline but a generic term covering a number of church leadership related studies. The question we are faced with is whether it can be a discipline, that is, an area of studies based on a phenomenology of the region we are calling ecclesial redemptive presence. A quick and tentative glance at ecclesial presence discloses that in addition to having historical and normative aspects, it has a world-transforming aspect. And this world-transforming aspect is in part something that is constitutive, that perdures through changing historical epochs, and at the same time is perpetually incarnated in the specific historical situation. Perhaps the central and perennial problem of grasping ecclesial presence lies here, how it can be redemptively pervasive of any and all social, political, and cultural spaces, without itself becoming identical with any of them and developing official and timeless ecclesial-political institutions. This problem and theme is the province of practical theology. Ecclesiology in the narrower sense and themes of the church, its ministries, and tasks of ministry should have their thematization within this larger theme of the world-transforming character of ecclesiality.

This proposal suggests at least the following possible gains:

1. Because its unity is not the teleology of the clerical paradigm, it is a plan of theological study pertinent in any situation and not restricted to clergy education.
2. Because its teleological unity is theological understanding, it avoids the pragmatic temper constitutive of all strictly professional education and restores to clergy education itself what has been so long absent—theology as a personal/existential *habitus*.
3. Because praxis is not identified with professional tasks but with world transformation, it permits the thematization of the actual, concrete political situationality in theological study, not as an autonomous theme, but in correspondance to ecclesial, redemptive presence.
4. It addresses the problem of the severing of the old practical theology from its theological matrix by making clerical studies subject to a discipline, practical theology, rooted in the world-transforming aspect of ecclesia.
5. It suggests a way of retaining the independence of existing religious and historical scholarship and of the critical principle and yet showing their structural connection with each other as disciplines of ecclesial presence.
6. It is flexible enough that it need not be identified with some one denominational, sectarian approach, but can receive the values and emphases of a denominational tradition.
7. Although its thematizing of world-transformation founds a discipline, practical theology, this is by no means a practice in contrast to theory, since the phenomenology of ecclesial redemptive presence does not yield aspects of that region, some of which are theory and others of which are practice.

NOTES

1. That *theologia* was something practical was self-evident to almost all parties in the scholastic theologies of Protestantism. Even the very high scholastics like Turretin saw theology as a *habitus* or wisdom, not just a school discipline. And yet the German pietists protested strongly against these understandings at the end of the seventeenth century. The problem was that the scholastics, while they viewed theology as an actual knowledge, treated it as

a parallel to ordinary knowledge. Therefore, this knowledge had a principium (Scripture) and various "causes" (efficient, material, final). Thus, though practical in that God was its true subject matter, the account of the theology as knowledge was very objectivist, formulated in such a way as to pertain to correct understandings of Scripture. And this opened the door to separating theology, even as a practical *habitus,* from piety. The pietist reform insisted also that theology was "practical," but in the sense of something that produced *Seligkeit,* pious happiness.

2. For instance, Hyperius (Andreas Gerhard), *De Theologo,* 1556; Alsted, *Praecognita,* 1614; Polänus, *Syntagma theologiae christianae,* 1616.

3. The two fullest accounts of the rise of theology as a discipline are Yves Congar, *The History of Theology,* trans. H. Guthrie (New York: Doubleday, 1968); and Gillian Evans, *Old Arts and New Technology: The Beginnings of Theology as an Academic Discipline* (Oxford: Clarendon, 1910). But see also F. Kattenbush's study, "Die Entstehung einer christliche Theologie," *Zeitschrift der Theologie und Kirche* (NF), vol. 11, 1930.

4. Two good accounts of the "new" universities in eighteenth-century Germany are found in F. Paulsen, *The German Universities,* trans F. Thilly (New York: Scribner, 1906); and Phillip Schaff, *Germany: Its Universities, Theology, and Religion* (New York: Sheldon, Blakeman, 1957).

5. In Bernard Lonergan's scheme of the "functional specialties" of theology, interpretation appears to be the closest item to what I am calling theology/*habitus.* See *Method in Theology* (New York: Herder and Herder, 1972), chap. 7.

6. The State's role in presiding over the higher faculties of the university and constituting the environment in which the pertinent institutions occur is articulated by Schleiermacher in his 1808 essay, "Gelegentliche Gedanken über Universitäten im deutschen Sinn."

7. A brief but excellent recent history of practical theology is the essay by Jurgen Henkys, "Die Praktische Theologie" (Einführung) in the *Handbuch der Praktische Theologie,* ed. H. Ammer, vol. 1 (Berlin, 1975).

8. See Friedrich Schleiermacher, *Brief Outline of the Study of Theology,* trans. T. Tice (Atlanta, GA: John Knox, 1977), part 3.

9. These definitions come from Phillip Schaff, *Theological Propaedeutic* (New York: Scribner, 1916), p. 448; and from Tholuck's *Theological Encyclopedia and Methodology,* trans. E. A. Park, in *Bibliotheca Sacra,* vol. 11, 1844, p. 726.

10. This is Johann Metz's criticism of traditional Christian theology and, by implication, of practical theology. According to Metz, if theology has in view the social and political situation at all, it cannot help but be a criticism of middle-class religion and its way of remembering the tradition. See *Faith in History and Society: Toward a Practical Fundamental Theology* (New York: Seabury, 1980).

3. Schleiermacher's Vision for Theology

JOHN E. BURKHART

WHEN Friedrich Schleiermacher (1768–1834) was appointed Professor Extraordinary of Theology and Philosophy at Halle in 1804, theological education was in its traditional disarray. Then, as now, the so-called theological disciplines were several and various; and the theological curriculum was a relatively incoherent conglomerate of diverse specialities. Is there nothing new under the sun? Perhaps more innovative than Koheleth, however, Schleiermacher was unwilling to acquiesce that "what has been done is what will be done" and he began to envision a new sequence and integration in the study of theology. A result, of course, is his now classic (but still neglected?) encyclopedia of theological studies, *Kurze Darstellung des theologischen Studiums* (*Brief Outline of the Study of Theology*), published in 1811 and revised in 1830.[1] The *Brief Outline* was composed as an introductory guide for theological students, to help them in understanding the purpose, significance, and interrelationships of the various parts of theological studies. As a formal encyclopedia, it is remarkably concise and eminently instructive; as a magisterial contribution from a theological genius, it surely deserves and worthily repays careful scrutiny.

Theology and Its Three Parts

For Schleiermacher, theology is "a positive science" (*eine positive Wissenschaft*), whose diverse and constituent parts are united by their common relationships to Christianity. Consequently, the practical task of guiding the Christian church both unites the several disciplines and makes them theological. Not every religion develops a theology, but Christianity does because it is communicated by ideas as well as by actions; and it is historically extensive, embracing many cultures and languages. Hence, among Christians, theology is a necessity for all who would undertake to guide the church. Thus, "just as that multifarious knowledge is combined into a theological whole only in the service of a definite interest in Christianity, so this interest in Christianity can likewise only manifest itself appropriately by assimilating that knowledge." Therefore, a balance must be sought, uniting an "ecclesial interest" (*kirchliches Interesse*) with a "scientific spirit" (*wissenschaftlicher Geist*). Parenthetically, it is surely worth note that Schleiermacher's understanding of Christianity, indeed of religion itself, is so irreducibly social that he tends to use "ecclesial interest" and "religious interest" interchangeably! Thus, according to Schleiermacher, theology is an intellectual activity undertaken by interested persons using scientific methods and its fundamental task is simply the task of understanding what Christianity is.

As Schleiermacher defines theology, he understands it to be composed of three constituent parts: philosophical theology, historical theology, and practical theology. For him, the three parts are interdependent and yet have a sequential relationship. According to the 1811 edition of the *Brief Outline,* philosophical theology is the "root" (*Wurzel*), historical theology is the "body" (*Körper*), and practical theology is the "crown" (*Krone*). The image, obviously, is vertical, and it suggests the integrity of a flourishing tree. Thus, although one could begin with any part, and the parts are truly interdependent, "the most natural order" (*die natürlichste Ordnung*) is from philosophical theology, through historical theology, to practical theology. This order, incidentally, may represent something of an ancient hierarchy—from pure science to mere technology, from the universal to the particular, from the theoretical to the applied (perhaps paralleled in the modern university's pecking order, where mathematicians look down on physicists, who look down on engineers, who look down on contractors and janitors). But, for Schleiermacher, at least, it is moderated by his recognition of the interdependence of the various parts of theological study, by his insistence upon a unity of the scientific spirit and ecclesial interest in each part, and by his profound emphasis upon historical theology as the actual corpus of theological study. Consequently, unlike a Neoplatonic rejoicing when matter is decently thin and studies are properly contemplative, Schleiermacher's proposed theological curriculum is directed towards what happens in the churches. For him, theological studies have no other reason for being. Indeed, unless they share some practical concern for ecclesial Christianity, they are not even theological!

For Schleiermacher, since the definition of Christianity can neither be deduced from general principles nor be derived empirically, philosophical theology has a critical function. It uses historical criticism to determine what Christianity truly is. Apologetics and polemics are the two fundamental divisions of philosophical theology. The task of apologetics is determination of the distinctive character of Christianity among the religions of the world. It is scientific in a definitional sense, since it seeks to describe the specific "essence of Christianity" (*Wesen des Christentums*) by defining the Christian *differentia* within the *genus* of religion. Its functions are wholly outward, as it develops the critical definition of what is truly Christian against those hostilities that arise from misunderstandings. The task of polemics is wholly inward, as attention is turned to the diagnosis of diseases in doctrine and/or polity. Polemics criticizes heresies and schisms. Of necessity, philosophical theology as such both presupposes the results of historical theology and also lays a theological foundation for the work of historical theology. Thus, whether through apologetics or through polemics, whether looking outward or inward, philosophical theology seeks to ascertain the essence of Christianity. The term "essence," by the way, should not be misunderstood. Schleiermacher does not understand Christianity statically. Indeed, for him, Christianity is a fundamentally historical reality. Always expressed in a living community, it is a "becoming" (*ein Werdendes*) in which the actual present grows as the fruit of the past and as the seed of the future.[2] Christianity is always a reality in process. In fact, perhaps the most significant contribution of philosophical theology, according to Schleiermacher, is the clarity with which it reveals the essentially historical character of Christianity.

Historical theology, therefore, precisely because of the "historical" character of Christianity, is hailed as the true body of theological study; and, not surprisingly, it occupies more than half of the pages (and propositions) of the *Brief Outline*. As Schleiermacher discusses historical theology, it becomes clear that the very phrase "historical theology" embodies an ambiguity inherent in all theological studies. As "historical," it is simply part of the modern secular studies of history and is therefore properly subject to all of the established principles of historical research; but as "theological," it brings interests and commitments that cause it to understand the career of Christianity as a particular historical "totality" (*Ganzes*) in which something genuinely new and definitive has arisen and is still being experienced. Consequently, historical theology is not simply concerned with the past, as if understanding the past were an end in itself; nor is it simply concerned with the impact of the past upon the present, as if understanding the present were an end in itself. It is interested in understanding a normative past and the impact of that past upon the developing career of that past into the present—in order to make a difference in the as yet unrealized future of that past. The true interests of historical theology are eminently practical. For Schleiermacher, history is not really understood until it is studied, with religious interest and critical scholarship, in order to act historically!

For Schleiermacher, therefore, the appropriate divisions of historical theology are exegetical theology, church history, and the historical knowledge of the present situation of Christianity. Exegetical theology is given the task of understanding those canonical documents deriving from earliest Christianity. These documents are normative precisely because they give witness to those original expressions of Christianity in which its authentic distinctiveness is most clearly revealed. In his view, by the way, the study of the Old Testament is ancillary to the study of the New, a view in which he may reveal himself to be more Lutheran than Reformed. In any event, in understanding Scripture, a "personal interest in Christianity" is to be united with a "philo-

logical spirit and art." According to Schleiermacher, those who
interpret the New Testament without scholarly skills only produce "disorder" (*Verwirrung*); and those who interpret the New
Testament without a personal interest in Christianity can only be
understood as antagonistic to it, since it, simply as literature,
lacks sufficient "linguistic importance" (*sprachliche Wichtig-
keit*) to engage the "art" (*Kunst*) of specialists. Parenthetically,
it should be noted that Schleiermacher himself occupied his considerable philological skills in translating Plato into German.

Church history studies the whole career of Christianity until
now, with particular interest in tracing the ways in which the
Christian community has been affected by the consequences of
its own actions and as a consequence of various other influences.
For example, church history studies how the course of Christianity's *life* has been affected by political circumstances and how its
doctrine has been affected by philosophical views. However,
while the tasks of historical study are endless, such study is never
an end in itself. "Nothing is more fruitless than a piling up of
historical learning which neither serves any practical purpose nor
offers anything for the use of others in its presentation."

For Schleiermacher, dogmatic theology is an aspect of historical theology, since it expresses historical knowledge of the present situation of Christianity. The dogmatic theologian articulates the Christian faith in relation to a particular historical
moment, avoiding the one-sidedness of either theological anti-
quarianism or traditionless innovation—since every historical
moment inevitably unites change with continuity. The present
should not be sundered from the past; nor should the past be
allowed to stifle the present. Furthermore, for Schleiermacher,
dogmatic theology should perhaps no longer be separated into its
"theoretical side" of doctrine and its "practical side" of ethics.
Such separations have worked to the impoverishment of both
doctrine and ethics, with doctrine becoming lifeless propositions
and ethics becoming external prescriptions. Hence, in his reading
of Christianity, theory and practice are, after all, simply inseparable sides of an integral reality.

Schleiermacher concludes his overview of historical theology
by turning to what he calls "church statistics" (*die kirchliche*

Statistik). He sees it as a new and developing field of study, devoted to the study of the whole situation of Christianity in the present. Indeed, as he admits, even dogmatics is really only an aspect of it and has been given a distinct place only because it lends itself to special treatment. And, it may be noted, from some perspectives, what he calls church statistics might be thought of as practical theology. Indeed, the line between the historical and the practical may prove as difficult to draw as was the line between the philosophical and the historical. Actually, the difficulty is enhanced precisely because Schleiermacher has the wisdom to think doctrine and ethics together. Yet, even within his discussion of dogmatics itself, perhaps the real clue to his understanding of the relation between theory and practice is anchored in his profound persuasion that a truly theological handling of doctrine is not possible "without personal conviction" (*ohne eigene Überzeugung*). For him, the unconvinced person who deals with doctrine,

> though he might well provide a report on it, and even on the manner in which the ordered structure of the doctrine is conceived, cannot establish the truth of this structure through the disposition he makes of it. Yet it is only this latter factor which makes the treatment dogmatic.[3]

In effect, therefore, and quite crucially for Schleiermacher, studies (of whatever subject matter) become theological through the use made of them. The question, fundamentally, is not so much of their content as it is of their use. Therefore, perhaps never before or since has theology been understood more practically than here.

In his own *Brief Outline*, however, Schleiermacher's actual discussion of "practical theology" does come as something of an anticlimax. It is, in a word, sketchy. Of course, as he notes, there were not too many good models to follow, for much of the earlier work in practical theology had been "very uneven" (*sehr ungleich*). Despite this, nonetheless, the real difficulty may reside in the way he defines and delineates the disciplines. For Schleiermacher, insofar as philosophical and historical theology have done their work properly and sufficiently, nothing seriously theoretical remains to be done. Practical theology is practical, not theoretical. In a word, he seem to have no theory for practical theology. Its tasks, which are tasks of application, are given it from philosophical and historical theology. It deals with "applied" Christianity. In his view, philosophical and historical theology can and should describe and understand the essence of Christianity and its historical actuality. Their dialectic discovers the discrepancy between what Christianity should become and what in fact it actually is. Practical theology, therefore, simply studies and indicates the appropriate rules, procedures, and methods to be used in overcoming the gap between the ideal and the actual. Its task is not hermeneutical but technological. Indeed, for Schleiermacher, practical theology is basically a "technology" (*Technik*).

Nevertheless, despite the limitations he places upon practical theology definitionally, his own discussions of it are instructive, and they wisely exemplify his own conviction that the "most appropriate methods will occur to the person whose historical basis for living in the present is the deepest and most diversified." Consequently, for him, methods, rules, and techniques are finally not enough. What really matters—whether in historical interpretation or in the care of souls—is what he characterizes in such words as "art" (*Kunst*), "talent" (*Talent*), and "interior disposition (*innere Beschaffenheit*). For him, theological studies are at best only equipment for ministry. The indispensable heart of ministry is to be found, not in philosophical insight, in historical knowledge, or in practical skill, but in those gifted persons whose faith and learning unite and grow into passionate wisdom; and in such persons he finally plants the hope that even the historic antagonisms between Protestants and Roman Catholics may be overcome.

Unity, Sequence, and Purpose of Theological Studies

Schleiermacher's *Brief Outline* is an extraordinary document, comprehensive in vision and suffused with insight. Amid the vast literature on the purpose and character of theological studies, it surely remains as the indisputable classic; and for those who would understand what they are doing in theological education, it continues as an unparalleled partner in dialogue. It is cogent and provocative, instructive, and enticingly visionary. In some ways, therefore, we may have reason to share the judgment, expressed by Schleiermacher's friend Friedrich Lücke (1791–1855), that the *Brief Outline*

contains a theology of the future rather than of the present. In this sense it is, to a certain extent, a truly prophetic work, which, upon the supposition of a vital progress in our science and our church, will, as time advances, meet with increasing fulfillment.[4]

In any event, we can agree with B. A. Gerrish that the *Brief Outline* is a "revolutionary manifesto," especially in its "turn to the historical."[5] For Schleiermacher, it is history that makes theological studies necessary. His own historical consciousness is profound. Consequently, those who share that consciousness may now wish to inquire whether and in what ways his vision is authentically appropriate for our time.

Any informed assessment of Schleiermacher's *Brief Outline* should, obviously, take account of his own intention, expressed in his preface, to direct students' "attention to matters of form, so that they may better apprehend the significance of the particular parts and their interrelation." Given this integrative intention, his success is manifest and compelling. He does manage, and in a measure that few have even attempted, to integrate quite disparate enterprises into a coherent *unity*. Inspired by this theological conviction that "everything is to be understood in the fullness of its relations" (*alles im Zusammenhang verstanden werden soll*), he seeks and finds, envisions and depicts an integral logic that sees theology as a unified science, composed of its philosophical, historical, and practical parts and unified in such a way that the normative, descriptive, and prescriptive tasks cannot finally be separated from each other. Consequently, he is convinced that the various specialities are genuinely interdependent, and that the specialists in each field can comprehend even their own fields only insofar as they understand their relationships to the other fields. Thus, without some general theological understanding, specialists simply exist incommunicado. Therefore, although he clearly understands and even stresses the importance of specialities and specialists, Schleiermacher poses the continuing question whether any isolated speciality (or specialist) is truly a part of theological studies.

Furthermore, he understands the unity of theology to imply some appropriate *sequence*. Unlike those theological encyclopedias that go around in circles (*en kyklios!*) simply describing a variety of disciplines *seriatim,* Schleiermacher attends to questions of proper sequence. Thus, while he is himself persuaded that the various theological disciplines are interdependent (and are therefore amenable to a variety of sequences), it was, according to his preface, the matter of order that initially prompted him to compose his own *Brief Outline.* For him, as *The Christian Faith* abundantly demonstrates, *viewpoint implies sequence;* and he believes that the movement from philosophical, through historical, to practical theology is not only logical but chronological. Schleiermacher, therefore, poses the continuing question whether theological studies are sequential, and what the most appropriate sequence is.

Schleiermacher, of course, derived his own sequence from his convictions about the *purpose* of theological study. For him, the purpose was the intellectual formation of leadership for the Christian churches. Theology, for him, is a positive science, with its component parts ordered toward the practical task of ministry. Theological studies are purposeful. They are not ends in themselves. That they simply are, or that they traditionally have been, is not in itself sufficient reason for their existence or continuance. Their rationale is in their use. Rooted in the essence of Christianity as determined by philosophical theology, and embodied in the tradition as interpreted by historical theology, they are crowned in ecclesiastical activities as deliberated by practical theology. For Schleiermacher, theological studies, like other professional studies (such as law or medicine), have their reason for being in their public function. For him, they are the indispensable preparation for wise leadership in the churches. Nevertheless, despite the clerical paradigm (a paradigm, incidentally, which may itself simply be a consequence of Schleiermacher's own historical circumstances), Schleiermacher poses the continuing question whether theological studies are purposeful and what gives them any real reason for being. Thus, it is surely the measure of Schleiermacher's achievement that his *Brief Outline* has unforgettably posed the continuing question of the unity, sequence, and purpose of theological studies.

Strength and Weakness of the *Brief Outline*

Perhaps the major strength of Schleiermacher's *Brief Outline* is his profound insight that studies, any studies, become explicitly theological through the theological interest brought to them. For him, no studies are intrinsically beyond the realm of theological interest; and, conversely, no studies can simply be assumed to be theological, merely because of their supposedly theological subject matter. In principle, therefore, sociology is no less deserving than patristics as a suitable candidate for inclusion among truly theological studies. The criterion for inclusion or exclusion is *use,* as use derives from personal or ecclesial interest. Given such an insight, it may be noted, the possible consequences for theological curriculum building (or demolition) are immense, stretching far beyond the imagination even of so creative theologian as Schleiermacher.

Schleiermacher's insight, of course, is quite fundamental to his theology. His answer to the scientific naturalism of his time was neither deistic nor supranaturalistic. God is neither an absentee landlord nor a miraculous meddler. There are no fixed lines between sacred and secular, since God is the ground of all reality. Thus, for example, as Schleiermacher puts it in the *Speeches,* "miracle" (*Wunder*)

is simply the religious name for event. Every event, even the most natural and usual, becomes a miracle, as soon as the religious view of it can be the dominant. To me all is miracle.[6]

Consequently, for Schleiermacher, theology is not a matter of seeing some special realities, but of seeing some ordinary realities differently. Theology is in the eye of the beholder. Thus, historical theology is a purposeful conjoining of historical and theological interests. Obviously the rules of historical inquiry apply to all (Schleiermacher is not a fideistic obscurantist); but the secular historian's "facts" are for Schleiermacher both facts and faith. Furthermore, whenever any knowledge, even of traditionally "sacred" matters, is acquired apart from "ecclesial interest," it "ceases to be theological and devolves to those sciences to which it belongs according to its varied content."

In Schleiermacher, New Testament studies afford an admirable case in point. As a Greek scholar of no mean distinction, Schleiermacher, on grounds of philosophical kinship and philological interest, translated Plato in German. Translating Plato was intellectually and personally exciting, as it drew upon his immense philological interests and skills. And, precisely as a Greek scholar, he could not imagine why anyone who was a Greek scholar would, simply as a scholar, bother with the New Testament, "since this book rates far behind other writings in linguistic importance." Indeed, simply as a scholar, even the scholarly abilities of those who do bother—apart from some interest given by faith—seem suspect to him. Nevertheless, as a devoted Christian, Schleiermacher deems the study of the New Testament as quite indispensable; and it is, for him, deserving of and served by the most rigorous historical scrutiny. But, notice, the scrutiny is no longer an end or delight in itself. It serves, in all its rigor, some purpose. Interest makes the difference.

Perhaps the major weakness or defect in Schleiermacher's *Brief Outline* is his failure to think through the implications of his major strength. He recognizes fully, as had Augustine and Anselm and others before him, that there is no true understanding apart from believing. *Credo ut intelligam.* Believing affects thinking, not to constrict or shackle it (as the Enlightenment objectivists often suppose), but to enlighten and empower it. Faith gives reason reasons for being. Nevertheless, what Schleiermacher fails to notice or understand in any effective way is that if believing affects thinking, practice influences theory.

Consequently, even though he recognizes and even stresses the interdependence of philosophical, historical, and practical theology, their relations are asymmetrical. To be sure, philosophical and historical theology clarify and correct each other, and both share practical interests. Indeed, apologetics reminds practical theology of the ecumenical prospects and dogmatics gives norms for popular communications. And. to a remarkable degree, practical theology is ingredient in Schleiermacher's emphasis upon "use" as the criterion for understanding studies as being "theological," so that in him, as in few others, practical theology is the "crown." Nonetheless, despite all this, for whatever reasons, in Schleiermacher practical theology does not affect philosophical or historical theology. For him, the concourse between theory and practice is a one-way street.

Thus, Schleiermacher reveals sound instincts in describing practical theology as theological; and he is obviously correct in stressing the unitive, integral function of "task"; and he is surely right in suggesting that theology and life, reflection and action, should not be sundered; and he is doubtless wise in his recognition that the heart of the matter is not thoughts or techniques but persons; nevertheless, he sees practical theology, finally, as consisting in the consequences and applications derived from thought done elsewhere. Hence, it tends to technique. It is, to be sure, deliberative, but not really reflective. And its findings, such as they are, are never permitted to force philosophical or historical theology to reconsider. Thus, quite simply, while thought influences action, action does not really influence thought. In other terms, there is *lex credendi, lex orandi,* but no *lex orandi, lex credendi.* Or, while he is astute enough to recognize hermeneutically that historical understanding "is a talent, one which is developed in each person, through varying degrees, through the resources of his own historical life," he makes no systematic use of this wisdom as he delineates the theological disciplines. In his *Brief Outline,* acting remains subordinate to knowing. As he himself puts it in the introduction:

Accordingly, historical theology is the actual corpus of theological study, which is connected with science, as such, by means of philosophical theology and with the active Christian life by means of practical theology.

Thus, although Schleiermacher knows, and knows thoroughly, that thought itself can be transformative, he nevertheless does not come to realize that life itself can be illuminative. In a word, his own life and thought did not bring him to any systematic understanding of the interpretive dimensions of *praxis.*[7]

An Implicit Vision
We have examined Schleiermacher's *Brief Outline,* describing its structural understanding of theology as composed of three parts, noting its emphasis upon the unity, sequence, and purpose

of theological studies, and suggesting its strength and weakness. Nevertheless, beyond all this, there may yet be a compelling *vision* implicit, if not explicit, in what Schleiermacher has written; and that vision may lead even to a salutary revisioning of practical theology.

According to Schleiermacher, it should be remembered, history is vitally important; and, so long as history was not taken seriously and Christianity continued servilely under the dominance of Scripture and/or tradition, theology could still be equated with received doctrine, to be mindlessly transmitted and applied to quite stable and therefore predictable circumstances. For Schleiermacher, however, given the realities of history and historical consciousness, every theologian should "aim to sift and supplement what others have contributed. . . ."

Without such an effort, no matter how complete his information may be, he would be a mere carrier of tradition—the lowest rank of all the activities open to a person, and the least significant.

For Schleiermacher, it is the historical reality of change that makes genuine theology possible and necessary. We are historical beings, living in history, shaped and changed by it. Therefore, the understanding of the Christian tradition in ever changing circumstances is the heart of theological activity. Indeed, for him, "the function of leadership in the Church can only be adequately performed on the basis of a highly developed consciousness of history." Consequently, his *Brief Outline* is replete with discussions of hermeneutics, interpretation, and understanding— words and interests that flow naturally from historical consciousness. Thus, although his discussions of "practical theology," unfortunately, make little or no use of these terms, it may be mentioned that at one point (in section 265) the task of "application" is nuanced so that it requires "rules of art" (*Kunstregeln*). The reference (explicitly made to section 132) is to hermeneutics as the "art" (*Kunst*) of understanding. Here Schleiermacher gives at least a hint of thinking practical theology itself to be a theological activity of *understanding*.

Furthermore, as his rethinking of the relations between dogmatics and ethics (in sections 223–231) suggests, theological reflections upon thought and action are not finally separable. The "theoretical" and the "practical" are simply distinguishable "sides" of a single reality. "Rules for the Christian life are also theoretical propositions" (*die christlichen Lebensregeln sind auch theoretische Sätze*). Something of a direction that practical theology might take may be envisioned in Schleiermacher's attention to the historical present as composed of "dogmatic theology" and "church statistics." For him, the present situation is not fully understood apart from knowledge "of the societal situation" (*des gesellschaftlichen Zustandes*). There is no genuine understanding of Christianity apart from interest and understanding in all of its life. Hence, Schleiermacher can be understood to have laid the basis for a genuinely theological practical theology; for, once practical theology is allowed tasks of understanding, actions as well as thoughts become properly matters for authentically theological concern. Consequently, within such a perspective, theology can begin to understand and interpret not only classic documents but classic behaviors as well. It can, as theology, attend as appropriately to liturgies and polities as it has to creeds and systems of thought; and, in a truly *incarnational* methodology, nothing can finally separate theory from practice or practice from theory. In Schleiermacher, the task of understanding and the understanding of task keep them together. Precisely because we are embodied creatures of history, theory and practice, while surely distinguishable, are inseparable. Action and thought, in reciprocal relation, are both generative of meaning and truth.

Finally, the vision of practical theology, perhaps already somewhat at work in Schleiermacher, is empowered by his *eschatological* impulses. His understanding is incarnational and eschatological. History, for him, has purpose, direction, and goal. Hence, the final "aim" (*Zweck*) of Christian theology "consists in representing its distinctive nature more authentically in every approaching instant of its history." Therefore, theology (he is here referring to apologetics) has the "divinatory" (*divinatorisch*) task of envisioning the ways in which present distortions (such as the separations between the churches) can be overcome.

Since in the evangelical Church both Church service and Church government are essentially conditioned by this Church's opposing position vis-à-vis the Roman Church, it is the highest accomplishment of practical theology to fashion both aspects of Church leadership in a way which shall be best adapted to the present state of this opposing position as compared with its culminating point historically.

For Schleiermacher, practical theology is, ultimately, the imaginative, futurist discipline *par excellence.* Its task is to understand—incarnationally, in theory and practice, using the resources of philosophical and historical theology, and itself contributing insight to them—the ways to overcome the distance between what human life is and what human life is meant to be. His vision, finally, is of a crowning and culminating speciality, dreaming and struggling, thinking and acting, acting and thinking, for the world to be reborn. Perhaps for Schleiermacher, and for us as well, practical theology thinks its distinctive theological tasks precisely by attending to what is required by its historical understanding of the goal of human life. Thinking truth in order to goodness and beauty, it asks concerning the "chief end" of humankind; and, perhaps alone among all the disciplines of theological studies, practical theology is truly eschatological.

NOTES

1. The critical edition, edited by Heinrich Scholz and published in 1910, has been reissued (Hildesheim: Georg Ohms, 1977). There is an English translation, *Brief Outline on the Study of Theology,* by Terrence N. Tice (Richmond, VA.: John Knox, 1966). The earlier English translation by William Farrer (Edinburgh: T. & T. Clark, 1850), including the "Reminiscences of Schleiermacher" by Friedrich Lücke, was reprinted (Lexington, KY: The American Theological Library Association, 1963). There is a summary of the *Brief Outline* by Ronald E. Sleeth, "Schleiermacher: "On Practical Theology—A Summary and an Analysis," *The Princeton Seminary Bulletin* 68 (Winter 1976): 41–49. For an overview of Schleiermacher, see Martin Redeker, *Schleiermacher: Life and Thought,* trans. John Wallhausser (Philadelphia: Fortress, 1973).
2. *Kurze Darstellung* (Scholz), p. 11. See B. A. Gerrish, *Tradition and the Modern World: Reformed Theology in the Nineteenth Century* (Chicago and London: University of Chicago Press), 1978, pp. 40, 196.
3. *Brief Outline* (Tice), p. 72; *Kurze Darstellung* (Scholz), p. 75.
4. Lücke, "Reminiscences" in *Brief Outline* (Farrer), p. 36.
5. Gerrish, *Tradition and the Modern World,* p. 40.
6. Friedrich Schleiermacher, *On Religion: Speeches to Its Cultured Despisers,* trans. John Oman (New York: Harper and Brothers, 1958), p. 88; *Über die Religion: Reden an die Gebildeten unter ihren Verächtern,* ed. Rudolf Otto (Göttingen: Vanderhoeck and Ruprecht, 1926), p. 74.
7. For an instructive discussion of praxis, see David Tracy, *Blessed Rage for*

Order: The New Pluralism in Theology (New York: Seabury, 1975), p. 243, where "*praxis* is correctly understood as the critical relationship between theory and practice whereby each is dialectically influenced and transformed by the other." See also David Tracy, "Theoria and Praxis: A Partial Response," *Theological Education* 17 (Spring 1981): 167–174; and Matthew L. Lamb, "The Theory-Praxis Relationship in Contemporary Christian Theologies," *The Catholic Theological Society of America, Proceedings* 31 (1976): 149–178. It may be noted that, according to his introduction, Schleiermacher wrote the *Brief Outline* because of the difficulty of lecturing from someone else's textbook. In this measure at least, his practice influenced his theory!

II

FOUNDATIONAL
PERSPECTIVES

4. The Foundations of Practical Theology

DAVID TRACY

MY AIM is to suggest one basic heuristic schema for practical theology as public theology. My claim is that practical theology attains its public character by articulating praxis criteria of human transformation as well as an explicitly theological ethic. The route to warrant that claim must, however, be a long, even a circuitous one.

A more direct route is, I believe, impossible. For the fact is all our experience, indeed all praxis, is theory-laden.[1] The first task of responsible reflection on practical theology, therefore, is to clarify the actual theories with which the practical theologian enters into the realm of praxis. Thereby we may see how praxis can sublate theory, neither merely apply nor simply negate it. The strategy of this long route is to resist two alternative models for practical theology. The first model in both classical and modern forms claims in effect, that practical theology merely applies theories worked out elsewhere (e.g., in systematic theology). In this model, as we shall see, praxis is misunderstood as mere practice, that is, as the development of technical means and skills for the application of theological theory. The theories are worked out earlier in what is called theology proper. Theological theories, in that model, are not really affected by any praxis, including the actual practice of ministry in all its forms. A second inadequate model (as in some forms of liberation theology) holds that praxis in effect does not sublate theory but simply negates it. Concrete actions and commitments to a particular cause supply all the criteria (the praxis criteria) necessary for truth in theology. This second model of practical theology, in my judgment, does correctly affirm the primacy of praxis for theory.

Still this form of the primacy-of-praxis position fails to see that all praxis, like all experience, is in fact theory-laden. Any failure to take account of this inevitable presence of theory in all praxis occasions a failure to note how praxis criteria actually relate to critical theory as theory's sublation, not its simple negation.

My attempt to develop an alternative model for practical theology will assume the following logical form. In a first section I will render explicit what earlier theological theories I assume as publicly warranted. These theories could be employed by practical theologians as they move into the arena of explicit concern with the further criteria of transformative praxis and ethical reflection. Chief among these critical theories are first, a theory on what theology *as theology* is; and, second, a theory on the criteria and character of the first two subdisciplines in theology (viz. fundamental and systematic theology). The theories with which practical theologians can begin their task are in fact those prior theories developed in fundamental and systematic theology. Those same theories, as I hope to show, receive their proper sublation through the transformation criteria and a theological ethics developed in practical theology itself.

The Nature of Theology
Theology is the discipline that articulates mutually critical correlations between the meaning and truth of an interpretation of the Christian fact and the meaning and truth of an interpretation of the contemporary situation. This general notion of theology, moreover, can be further distinguished into three subdisciplines: fundamental theology, systematic theology, and practical theology.[2] The logical spectrum for these subdisciplines is the spectrum from the relatively abstract (fundamental theology) to the concrete (practical theology). Each subdiscipline develops public criteria for its claims to meaning and truth. Those criteria also range from the necessary and abstract (transcendental or metaphysical) criteria of fundamental theology through the hermeneutical criteria of truth as disclosure and concealment in systematic theologies to the concrete praxis criteria of truth as personal, social, political, historical and natural transformation and

ethical reflection in practical theology. All three subdisciplines are needed to assure the presence of the full range of criteria necessary for the affirmation of the public character of theology's claims to meaning and truth.

Some initial clarification of the major elements in the general definition of theology are in order here. First, the phrase "mutually critical correlations" indicates that the theologian must allow for a full logical spectrum of possibilities.[3] That spectrum ranges from claims of identity (between the meaning and truth of the Christian fact and the contemporary situation) through claims for similarities-in-difference (analogies) or complementarities to claims of pure confrontation or nonidentity. Any option is logically possible in principle. Only the facts of the particular subject matter can decide the issue in each case. Hence the phrase "mutually critical correlations." The correlations, moreover, are between both the questions *and* responses of both phenomena, the Christian tradition and the contemporary situation, not simply "questions" from one pole and "responses" from the other.

Second, the word "interpreted," is also crucial for both the Christian fact and the contemporary situation, for the explicit insistence on the central role of interpretation in all theology indicates two principal factors. First of all, we do not receive either the Christian tradition or the contemporary situation in an immediate form. The claims of immediate self-consciousness of the Cartesian model have long since been exposed as illusory. We come to self-consciousness not immediately but mediately, that is, through the social and historical mediations of a particular culture as present principally in the concrete language that is, as we properly say, our "native" language. Neither Christianity nor the contemporary situation is present to us in immediate or static forms as objects-over-against-our-subjectivity. Both come to us in mediated and often unconscious forms, especially through verbal language and symbol. We must, therefore, mediate, translate, that is, interpret both realities.

It is also true that interpretation emerges as a particular problematic usually only when a specific tradition can no longer be

received or repeated with immediacy. So it was for the ancient
Stoics in relationship to the Greek and Roman religions. So it is
for Christians and Jews since the emergence of historical consciousness. To emphasize this double need for interpretation in
our situation (and, therefore, for an appropriate theory of interpretation) at every stage of theology is crucial. This hermeneutical element allows us to see that any theology should be historically conscious of its own problematic status and, therefore, its
own need to provide public criteria of meaning and truth for its
claims to continued attention by the wider public.

Third, the words "meaning and truth" may serve for the moment as heuristic terms to emphasize that theological "meaning
and truth" cannot be merely assumed. They must be shown and,
as far as possible, stated. More exactly, criteria to adjudicate all
claims to meaning and truth in the public forum should be rendered explicit at every stage of the process.

Fourth, the expression "the Christian fact" is intended to
serve two primary purposes. First, the word "fact" serves to remind us that Christianity is not something we invent. Christianity exists and demands rediscovery and interpretation—the latter
including retrieval, and critique and suspicion—but not inven-
tion. Second, the choice of the word "fact" (over alternatives like
message, kerygma, tradition) is also meant to remind us that the
Christian fact includes the whole range of classic texts, symbols,
events, persons, images, rituals, and practices from the New Testament forward (and, even retrospectively, the Hebrew scriptures now understood as the Christian Old Testament). Any interpreter of the Christian fact is likely to develop some selective
principle as the central clue or focal meaning for the whole. For
myself, that central clue is the event and person of Jesus Christ
as the decisive disclosure of the Christian construal of God, self,
and world. But any choice of either a central symbol (here the
symbol of the Christ; alternatively the Spirit, God, or humankind) must hold itself responsible to correctives from the full
range of symbols, texts, images, events, and so forth. Only then
is the full range of the Christian fact allowed to play its proper
hermeneutical role.

Fifth, the expression "the contemporary situation" is also intended to serve two roles. First, it serves to indicate that the situation is always already involved in any interpretation of any tradition (or, in Hans-Georg Gadamer's language, application is always involved in all interpretation).[4] I believe, with Gadamer, that "insofar as we understand at all we understand differently," that is, that there is no way simply to exclude the de facto presence of the history of the effects of tradition on our preunderstanding of our own situation. We can raise this reality of the operation of our preunderstanding in all interpretation to explicit consciousness—as here in the insistence that the contemporary situation is one of the two poles of Christian theology. Second, the expression "the contemporary situation" also reminds us of the actual pluralism of that situation. There are, in fact, several context-dependent analyses of the situation. There are several fundamental questions on these different interpretations of the situation that bear religious import (finitude, mortality, anxiety, fundamental trust, guilt, alienation, or oppression). Once again each interpreter will ordinarily choose one aspect of the situation for analysis. One may choose, for example, the crisis of cognitive claims for Christianity, the realities of alienation, privatization and oppression, the reality of massive human suffering in the world, the reality of the need to recognize the demands for a truly global culture, and so forth. That initial choice of the major problematic in the situation will also influence the choice of some fundamental question. That question in turn will influence and be influenced by the symbols from Christianity selected to interpret the Christian vision relevant to the situation. Yet this selectivity of problematic and question should, like the earlier selectivity of principal symbols, also hold itself responsible to the fuller pluralistic realities in the entire global situation and thereby to the full range of fundamental questions disclosed in that situation.

This general understanding of theology as the "mutually critical correlation of the meaning and truth of an interpretation of the Christian fact and the meaning and truth of an interpretation of the contemporary situation" serves as a general rubric informing all forms of authentically theological reflection. However, this general rubric can only receive its real specificity by becoming concretized into three basic subdisciplines in theology.

Fundamental Theology

Fundamental theology establishes its mutually critical correlations in an obviously public manner—by providing arguments for its positions available in principle to any attentive, intelligent, rational, and responsible human being. Fundamental theologies, therefore, are involved in a necessary abstraction from the concrete. More exactly, the fundamental theologian abstracts from any highly personal experience (including faith experience) in order to concentrate on an analysis of our common (as communal) human experience. This reflection, moreover, will take the form of providing public arguments on the three logically prior questions to any claim to publicness of any religious tradition. For the Christian tradition these questions are: Is a religious interpretation of our common human experience meaningful and true? Is a theistic interpretation of religion meaningful and true? Is a Christian interpretation of religious theism meaningful? The responses to these questions should then be correlated critically to the questions and responses of Christianity. The correlations, to repeat, allow for the full range of identity to similarity to analogy to nonidentity (or confrontation).

For example, there may be a claim to the virtual identity between our "common faith" and Christian faith. Or there may occur a more modest claim to real analogies (or similarities-in-difference). There may also be a claim to utter nonidentity between these two "faiths." Sometimes an understanding of the Christian tradition will challenge, even confront, an understanding of the secular culture on grounds acceptable in principle (i.e., public) to that culture, as when Christian fundamental theologies of secularity challenge secularist interpretations of that shared secularity. At other times the challenge or confrontation will work in the opposite direction, as in challenges to classical theism from modern process thought or challenges to exclusivist christologies or ecclesiologies from modern historical consciousness. The general method allows for both possibilities. Only the particular subject matter can provide the concrete candidates for the public resolution of any particular attempt at establishing mutually critical correlations.

In every case the issue in fundamental theology is to be argued on grounds public to all, that is, available in principle to all intelligent, rational, and responsible persons. Crucial to this position of fundamental theologies is, of course, a notion of reason that is more comprehensive than either classical deductivist models of reason or modern positivist notions of the strictly instrumental character of reason. Indeed, one of the crucial theories that any theologian carries into practical theology after exposure to fundamental theology is precisely the notion of a more comprehensive notion of reason itself.[5] It is that notion of reason—and it alone—that can finally warrant the kind of genuinely critical theory needed for critical reflection on praxis. More exactly, as we shall see later in this chapter, critical theory is critical precisely by allowing for a more comprehensive notion of reason that demands a grounding in the self-reflective and self-corrective nature of all inquiry. That self-reflective and self-corrective character is itself limited to the praxis of the *value* of critical theory for human emancipation. Insofar as this wider concept of reason (and, hence, of the possibility of critical theory) makes its case plausibly in fundamental theology, this will affect practical theology. More exactly, the practical theologian will enter the discussion on praxis with fully public warrants for religion and theism and public warrants, as well, for the public availability, in principle, of particular religious symbols and traditions.

However, as soon as we mention this last factor, we may also note that fundamental theology, although necessary, cannot suffice. The determination in fundamental theology of certain abstract, general, necessary criteria—that is, phenomenological and transcendental for religious language (as public limit-language and theistic language as the public referent-language for that limit-language)—provides necessary but not sufficient criteria. For the latter, on fundamental theology's own terms, we must see whether the particularity (including the particular vision of God, self, and world in the Christic vision) also bears a more concrete but no less public character. If fundamental theology alone operates, then particular religious traditions and the uncommon or paradigmatic religious events, symbols, and texts that inform those traditions are in danger of privatization. The particular religious traditions would be privatized in the sense that only our common human experience and only arguments related to that experience would count as resources for the wider public. The more comprehensive scope of reason initially established in fundamental theology would contract by providing only an irrational decisionism for the concrete particularity in religious traditions. But before accepting that fate, we must first study (from the viewpoint of fundamental theology) the distinct but related, the more concrete but, I shall argue, no less public claims to meaning and truth of systematic theologies.

Systematic Theology

Systematic theologies may be defined as interpretations of a particular religious tradition in and for a particular situation. The key is the notion of interpretation as providing both public meaning and truth. The interpreter need not fear that this understanding of systematics will lead to privatization and decisionism, if interpretation includes the following elements:

1. Every interpreter enters with some preunderstanding of the questions and thereby the responses of the text. Included in that preunderstanding is the history of the effects of a particular tradition or traditions (carried especially in language). Included as well is some sense of the applicability of these questions to the interpreter's situation.

2. Every classic text, event, image, or symbol bears its own claim to attention for the interpreter.[6] Insofar as the interpreter responds to the provocation of that claim, she or he enters into a conversation-as-dialogue with the now common questions and possible responses provoked by the text.

3. That conversation can be expanded to include the full arc of the entire hermeneutical process. Interpretation begins with an initial understanding provoked by the text. It moves forward through an explanation via some methods (formalist, structuralist, semiotic, and so forth) on how the sense of the text produces its referent as a possible-mode-of-being-in-the-world.[7] Interpretation concludes with some fuller understanding of this particular mode of being as a

genuinely possible one for human beings and thereby as genuinely public.

Even in this abbreviated form, it is worth noting that interpretation in this model is not a private but a public act. Indeed, insofar as the text, event, or symbol is some classic expression of the human spirit, the text itself achieves its publicness not despite but through its very particularity. Every classic work of art and every major religion is intensely particular in both origin and expression. Classics in both art and religion achieve their form of publicness not in spite of but in and through that very particularity.

The provocation of the interpreter's own particularity by the classic particularity of the text will assure that every authentic understanding of a classic will be both particular and public. Indeed, precisely as such, every true interpretation will necessarily be different. The truth of interpretation of the religious claims in systematic theology will prove to be the same kind of truth as that available from any realized experience of a classic work of art—the truth of some disclosure and concealment of an essential aspect of our existence (e.g., finitude). The criteria available are the same kind of criteria as those employed for art. These criteria include public (as communal) senses of taste and cultivation and public formal and even explanatory criteria for the work itself.

In the case of "systematic" theology, the theologian as interpreter of the classic symbols, events, texts, and images of a particular religious tradition will, therefore, be concerned to interpret the disclosive truth of the religious classics of the tradition by means of hermeneutical criteria analogous to those employed in literary criticism and aesthetic theory.

Moreover, the inevitable pluralism of readings of any classic will be guided by these same criteria into a public discussion of the relative adequacy or inadequacy of the different readings. That pluralism is not imposed on the process of interpretation but is itself grounded in the plurality operative in every classic text, symbol, image, and tradition as well as the plurality of situations or horizons of every interpreter. That fact of plurality will also lead to an insight into the inevitable cognitive and moral ambiguity that is also present in every classic, including every classic religious tradition. At that point the pluralism of readings becomes a tensive conflict of interpretations.

Because of that conflict, the theologian recognizes the need not only for a hermeneutics of retrieval of the classics but also a hermeneutics of both critique and suspicion for every religious and cultural tradition. Every great work of civilization, as Walter Benjamin reminds us, is also a work of barbarism. Every great religious tradition (as the prophetic-reformatory core of Judaism and Christianity should also remind us) has produced radically ambiguous effects. Consider, for example, the central symbol of Christianity, the Christ symbol. That symbol has produced in its history of effects not only the healing, disclosive, and transformative realities of genuine religious redemption for millions but sometimes has produced, unintentionally to be sure but no less fatally, anti-Semitism, sexism, class prejudice, racism, and an arrogant exclusivism.

The need, therefore, for both hermeneutics of retrieval and hermeneutics of critique-suspicion (indeed, often retrieval of half-forgotten or repressed aspects and classic memories of the tradition through critique and suspicion) is grounded in the realization that every disclosure of truth in every classic is at the same time a concealment. That same need is also warranted on inner-theological grounds. It is warranted by both the mystical and the prophetic strains in the Christian tradition insofar as both demand constant self-criticism and self-reform.

To speak of the hermeneutical character of systemic theology, in sum, is not to speak only of meaning but also of truth. That truth of the religious classics will prove distinctive yet genuinely analogous to the truth as both disclosure and concealment in the classic works of art. Systematic theology will develop, therefore, distinctive yet analogous criteria of relative adequacy for the interpretation of its religious classics. More importantly for our present purposes, these hermeneutical reflections, once united to a publicly defensible critical theory of the phenomenon of the classic, will challenge both the marginalization of art and the privatization of religion. Every classic work of art and every classic religious tradition can be honored as bearing public resources not despite but through their very particularity. The realm of symbolic interaction will recognize those classic particularities as not private but public. They remain public insofar as they function as disclosive of truths about our common situation.

Nor are these hermeneutical results without import for practical theology itself, for the more comprehensive notion of reason that the development of critical theory in practical theology needs for its reflections in praxis will now be expanded to include the disclosive and therefore public possibilities present in the classic symbols, texts, images, and so forth. The Cartesian temptation to believe that we understand with immediate self-consciousness will be challenged by the insight that we understand by understanding the mediations of the human spirit in all the classic works of our tradition. The Enlightenment temptation to believe that particular traditions are, by definition, particularist and traditionalist—in a word, private—will be challenged by the recognition that every classic tradition yields disclosive truth to anyone willing to risk interpreting it.

The classics need not be handed over to the classicists; tradition need not become the personal property of traditionalists. Even the authority of the classic texts, symbols, persons, and images can operate as the authority of persuasive disclosure, not authoritarian coercion. In short, the body public is enriched, not impoverished, by the disclosive realities of the classic religious traditions. The scope of reason is enlarged, not contracted, by an admission of the public/disclosive power of the symbols of a particular tradition—as the role of Reinhold Niebuhr or Paul Tillich in the wider public should already have reminded us.

From the beginning to the end of the entire hermeneutical process, moreover, authentic praxis is operative. In a manner analogous to the necessity for the praxis of the value of critical theory for the fundamental theologian, the systematic theologian, precisely as interpreter of the tradition, must ethically honor the complex and demanding praxis of authentic interpretation and its attendant criteria.[8] As interpreter of a pluralistic and ambiguous tradition, for example, the systematic theologian will admit and explicate the selectivity of the vision of the tradition employed. The interpreter will be open to further correction and revision from other interpretations, and from the correctives of the analysis of fundamental theology. The very praxis of interpretation will also open one to the further test of transformative praxis. The interpreter will be alert to the need for criteria for a responsible pluralism of readings and attentive to the need for hermeneutics of both retrieval and critique-suspicion.

Finally, the systematic theologian as interpreter of the religious classics of the tradition will also recognize that we are left, at the final moment of the interpretation, with a possible-mode-of-being-in-the-world. As possible, this vision is both disclosive and thereby public and applicable and thereby open to the test of application through praxis. As disclosive, the Christian vision, like any classic vision, is also in some sense transformative for the interpreter. As applicable, this vision is both grounded in praxis and open to a final test of its truth—the test of transformative praxis and critical theological ethical reflection. What Schleiermacher names the ethical moment following the hermeneutical moment, I here call the need for practical theology following the disclosive concreteness of systematic theology. With the necessary and abstract criteria of the fundamental theologian as well as the concrete hermeneutical criteria of disclosure, the practical theologian enters to perform a distinct task. That task, I repeat, is not simply to "apply" these theories and interpretations through skills and techniques. It is also not to forget them in the "blooming, buzzing confusion" of theory-laden experience and praxis. The task of practical theology, rather, is to test this vision and, in that testing, transform it. The question, therefore, recurs: What is practical theology and how does it achieve its proper publicness?

Practical Theology
As my previous comments indicate, I believe that the principal praxis criteria for practical theology are criteria of transformation and the principal theoretical criteria are those of a theological ethics related to that praxis. The rubric by means of which these complex criteria can be clarified is the distinction of theory and praxis. For the moment, let us consider *praxis* simply as

action, that is, as what one does or possibly or probably can do in concrete circumstances. To see more clearly the difficulties with the theory-praxis relationship in our own period (and thereby in practical theologies in our period) it is instructive to return first to the classical Aristotelian distinctions between *theoria, praxis,* and *techne.*[9]

For Aristotle, politics is continuous with ethics, the doctrine of the good and just life. Both politics and ethics refer to human action (or "doing"). They are guided as cognitive disciplines by the practical intent of developing a virtuous character and a moral-political order conducive to the development of virtue. Since both ethics and politics refer to moral praxis (which is, of course, changing and contingent), their cognitive status as disciplines can be related to neither theory (as unchanging *episteme*) nor production (as *poiesis* and *techne,* i.e., making, not doing). Ethics and politics, unlike metaphysics, must deal with the "more or less" or "in most cases." Ethics and politics, for Aristotle, do not develop metaphysical theories but critical reflections to encourage the capacity named *phronesis,* that is, prudent understanding of variable situations with a view as to what is to be done.

The history of the effects of these classical Aristotelian distinctions between *episteme* (theory), *praxis,* and *techne* in the modern period is both complex and still highly debatable. Even those moderns like myself who believe that the Aristotelian distinctions are retrievable in our situation must recognize that no single one of them can any longer be simply identified with the classical usage. For theory in our period is neither Aristoleian mimetic contemplation of the eternal and necessary divine order nor is theory modeled on the ideals of mathematical certainty and necessity of the *Posterior Analytic. Techne* in our period is not limited to the reproduction of the material conditions of existence through the traditional crafts (making) but has become a scientific technology. And *praxis* in our period cannot be limited to virtuous action of moral agents guided by the classical Greek models of the virtuous life.

Indeed, the crucial strife in our period is elsewhere. In theory, it is the strife between either positivist notions of theory or instrumentalist notions of the range of reason as purely technical versus critical theories. The latter term includes all those theories based on the self-corrective and self-reflective nature of inquiry and natural discourse and guided by an emancipatory thrust.[10] *Techne,* to repeat (as John Dewey saw with clarity), becomes, with modern technology, theory-laden. Hence any serious attempt to link techniques and values in our period (as in practical theologies) must demonstrate the interdependence of the values chosen and techniques that can be utilized for the fulfillment of these value-oriented needs and interests. For, as many forms of contemporary practical theology instinctively sense (with Dewey), value convictions will persist in a technological society only to the extent that they can be utilized to available or imaginable techniques for their realization.

Yet this instinctive sense of many forms of practical theology oriented to the development of skills and techniques (practice) often functions without Dewey's own insistence on the need for critical theories. These theories are needed, first, to show the interdependence of techniques and values. In practical theology, moreover, the theory most needed is a critical theory of a theological ethics that will ground those values in moral and religious *praxis,* not in *techne.* Indeed, I believe that it can be plausibly argued that the greatest shift in the modern period is not the shift from classical theory to either positivist or critical theory, nor the shift from classical *techne* (or craft) to modern theory-laden technology, but the shift (directly related to the earlier shifts in both theory and *techne*) of praxis itself. In some practical theologies, the consequences of this shift are nothing less than devastating, for praxis has often become mere *techne,* that is, technique, skill. Only techniques and skills are allowed to play a genuinely public role. Moral and religious praxis (indeed all needs and interests) have become privatized. Those techniques, moreover, are indeed theory-laden but too seldom explicitly related by critical theories to the desired needs, interests, and values (or moral and religious praxis). The result is that both the theological and the ethical critical theoretical components become, in effect, remainder concepts. We are left with public techniques but only private religious and moral values.

The marginalization of art and the privatization of religion addressed in systematic theology are now joined by the privatization (or, alternatively, the pure formalization) of ethics and the scientization of politics (or, alternatively, the depolitization of the entire public realm). Practical theology becomes public only in its development of techniques, whereas theory is either discarded altogether or assumed to bear a purely positivist or instrumentalist character. Praxis becomes either some form of private action by a particular group or praxis serves as a code word for some claim to privileged status for the practice of one particular group (the various successors of the "proletariat"). Worse still, praxis can become simply the development of techniques for the application of often unacknowledged theories worked out elsewhere than in the realm of praxis itself. The comprehensive notion of reason warranted both by fundamental theology's defense of critical theory and systematic theology's defense of the public/disclosive role of symbols from particular traditions is quietly disowned. Instead we seem left with a notion of reason that is unconsciously instrumentalist and a public realm ruled by an irrational decisionism among private visions.

I do not paint this rather bleak picture of the dilemma of practical theologies in our period in order to suggest a simple return to the classical distinctions of Aristotle. Although I continue to believe that important elements of the Aristolelian position are indeed retrievable for our situation, the fact is, pace Leo Strauss or, in theological ethics, Stanley Hauerwas, the classic route is not retrievable save through the kind of historical and social-scientific mediations effected by the Hegelian and Marxist traditions in Europe or the Peirce-Dewey tradition in North America.

What we can affirm with Aristotle and the classical tradition is that praxis is the action of moral agents guided by some goal of the good and virtuous life and directed to the development of a character possessing *phronesis* or practical wisdom. What we can also affirm in our period is, first, that praxis is mediated through a historical and social consciousness that needs explicit study; second, that praxis must be explicitly related to the techniques of modern technology in order to prove effective; and, third, that the goal of the good and virtuous life is itself a projected possibility for any agent.[11] We need, therefore, to interpret critically ideals of the future of the self, society, history, and nature. Those ideals may prove teleological in the sense of classical humanism, even utopian (including retrospective utopias like Eliade's) or eschatological. The introduction of this last word "eschatological" (i.e., visions of a promised *adventum* for the future) reminds us anew that any practical theology that is really a theology must include a public defense of the disclosive and transformative (and, therefore, public) theological construal of reality at every step of this complex process.

There can be, in short, a public discussion of models of human transformation, including religious models. There should also be a public discussion of critical ethical reflection upon those models, including explicitly and deliberately theological ethics. I assume, in short, that ethics is critical reflection on moral praxis and that moral praxis is always mediated through historical and social consciousness. This leads me to propose that *practical theology* is the mutually critical correlation of the interpreted theory and praxis of the Christian fact and the interpreted theory and praxis of the contemporary situation. If the correlation is indeed open to the full spectrum of claims to identity, analogy, and pure nonidentity, then the first step must be to see what major models of human transformation are available de facto and what criteria of responsible transformation can be responsibly argued for. The conversation should in principle include all those seeking a true consensus based on a comprehensive notion of reason and guided by various future ideals for the actualization of a shared emancipatory thrust of reason itself towards freedom. My more specific proposal includes the development of practical theology as a collaborative enterprise that includes four principal steps:

1. There would be, first, a collaborative exercise of the development of models of human transformation. Those models would be provided by psychology, social science, historical studies, cultural anthropology, philosophy, ecological theories, and religious studies and theologies. Those models would include both synchronic models (for example, structural models of developmental constants like those of Jean

Piaget, Bernard Lonergan, Lawrence Kohlberg, and James Fowler) as well as diachronic models of a critical analysis of degrees of relative adequacy of human transformation in different psychological, social, historical, and religious variables (for example, the models of Don Browning, H. Richard Niebuhr, Reinhold Niebuhr, and James Gustafson).

Practical theologians at this point in their task would attempt to develop mutually critical correlations of the relative adequacy (based on claims of transformation) of the alternative models, including the religious models.

2. A second step would develop, again on a collaborative basis, an analysis of the public claims to human transformation provided by different concrete ideals for the future. Once again, those ideals are various. There exist secular humanist ideals like those of Jürgen Habermas, secularist and systematic ones like .Thomas Luckmann's or B. F. Skinner's, utopian and futurist ones like Ernst Bloch's or Herbert Marcuse's, retrospective utopian candidates like Mircea Eliade's or Eric Voegelin's, or Jewish or Christian eschatological ideals (like those of the political and liberation theologians). Once again, those ideals would be tested collaboratively by their claims to human transformation. On that basis, they would be accorded different degrees of relative adequacy. It is important to emphasize that the latter praxis criteria of relative adequacy should themselves be critically related to the earlier criteria of coherence, adequacy, and disclosure developed in fundamental and systematic theology for any final judgment of relative adequacy. However, a collaborative development of judgments of relative adequacy in terms of possibilities of human transformation in practical theology is an appropriate one justified by the very comprehensive notion of reason established in fundamental and systematic theologies themselves.

3. The hermeneutical element in both these first two steps in practical theology, moreover, is worth emphasizing. The hermeneutical character of all understanding is intensified, not lessened by any attempt to interpret historically and socially mediated models of human transformation. More-

over, as the pluralism and ambiguity in all classics show, every symbol, tradition, and text is both likely to yield a plurality of relatively adequate interpretations and is likely to bear its own train of both cognitive and moral ambiguity. When that moral ambiguity becomes systematic distortion, moreover, the need for critical theories to inform hermeneutics of suspicion is urgent. Those critical theories are genuinely critical in the sense specified above. Examples include psychoanalysis on the individual level, ideology critique on the social, cultural, and historical levels, genealogical analysis of values on the cultural level and, in the religions, both the mystical discernment traditions and the prophetic critique traditions. All operate as authentic hermeneutics of suspicion. The major task of critical theory here will be to unmask the systematic distortions in the person, social, cultural, historical, and religious models of human transformation. A subsidiary task will be to unmask the systematic distortions in the critical theories informing these hermeneutics of suspicion themselves—as in feminist critical theoretical analyses of both classical Freudian psychoanalysis and prophetic Christianity.

4. In sum, these first three collaborative steps for practical theology will be involved in disciplined reflection upon the possible mutually critical correlations obtaining between secular models of moral praxis with an emancipatory thrust and Christian faith praxis. A basic description of Christian faith praxis in terms of praxis, I suggest, is: faith working through justice and love and guided by the hope of a genuinely eschatological ideal. Yet as soon as one sees this need for critical correlation in terms of models of transformative praxis one can also see the necessity for explicit ethical reflection as the fourth and final step of practical theology. To repeat, I understand ethical reflection to be critical theoretical reflection upon moral praxis. In this model, ethical reflection depends on a hermeneutics (or phenomenological description) of moral praxis itself (as in the first three steps). Yet then ethical reflection provides its own critical theoretical reflection upon a now interpreted and phenomenologically described moral praxis.

Without explicitly ethical reflection a practical theology employing the first three steps could be left with a purely dispositional ethics, modeled on possibilities of human transformation. The difficulty with a purely dispositional ethic is not, of course, that it is unnecessary but that it is insufficient. A purely dispositional ethic is especially insufficient in a situation like the modern one where the danger of privatization affects all moral positions and can render dispositions nondiscussable. In sum, a further collaborative effort must ensue. The effort, from the viewpoint of practical theology, is the need to develop mutually critical correlations between secular critical ethical theories grounded in moral praxis and religious and theological critical ethical theories grounded in moral and religious praxis. All the usual public candidates for the most relatively adequate ethical theory (deontological, teleological, axiological, mixed theories, etc.) should be honored as authentic conversation partners for the arguments on ethical issues.

Some explicit development and, I admit, selectivity of ethical principles, rules, and norms is likely to occur, but any selectivity will occur, in this model, in the fully public realm of arguments on relative adequacy. A theological ethic that is both genuinely theological and authentically ethical will, therefore, attempt to establish mutually critical correlations between its theological ethic and alternative secular ethics. The theological character of the ethic will be developed, first, from the particular theological construal of reality established in fundamental and systematic theologies as the latter have been tested (and possibly transformed) by the transformation criteria of the first three steps of practical theology. All these earlier analyses, to repeat, may themselves again be transformed by a critical theological ethical theory explicitly related to earlier interpretations of moral and religious praxis. Insofar as those critical theories can move past a purely dispositional ethic to develop critical theoretical principles, norms, and rules appropriate to its theoretical character and its theological norms, then a Christian theological ethic proper (both personal and social) could, in principle, be developed as the final collaborative step in practical theology.

If this model for practical theology seems plausible, then it becomes clear that a major discipline needed for practical theology is theological ethics. Yet it is important to recall that, in this model at least, a theological ethics can perform its task with relative adequacy only if it is explicitly related to an interpretation of historically and socially mediated praxis—and, therefore, to the hermeneutical disciplines of history and the social sciences. Moreover, this model of practical theology can only perform its task well in critical relationship to the criteria and results of fundamental and systematic theology. Just as the latter need the criteria of transformative praxis for their correction, so too practical theology needs the correctives of the critical theories (including the transcendental theories) of fundamental theology and the disclosive hermeneutics of systematic theology.

Recall, for example, the ease with which some practical theologies use the model of Exodus for interpreting God's actions in history. That model may well be transformative. Yet it is also necessary to ask what coherent metaphysical account of God's action in history informs that model. If that model is metaphysically incoherent, the transformations may remain real but, at best, relatively inadequate theologically. At worst this kind of practical theology will enjoy a short-lived victory over secular (e.g., Marxist) interpretations. The spectrum remains that of the abstract to the concrete. From the relative abstraction of the understanding of God as the one strictly necessary individual (in fundamental theology) to the greater concreteness of a Christic envisionment of God as the comprehensible-incomprehensible, revealed and hidden God of pure unbounded love (in systematic theology) to an understanding of God's transformative action in the self, society, and history in the transformative praxis of faith-working-through-love and justice and guided by the hope of God's eschatological future (in practical theology), the collaborative character of all theology (whether fundamental, systematic, or practical) should be clear. There is no one set of criteria to decide all these issues. There are, rather, different sets of relevant criteria applicable to the various aspects abstracted from the concrete whole that is theology.

Only when a comprehensive notion of reason is allowed will these criteria operate in a genuinely public manner. For only then will the disciplined reflection that all theology must be yield its contributions to a revitalized public realm. Nor is it the case that the criteria (always criteria of relative adequacy) in fundamental, systematic, and practical theologies are without any historical warrants. Returning for one final time to Aristotle, I claim that the criteria I argue for are analogous to his own. The criteria of fundamental theology are analogous to what Aristotle named dialectic and metaphysics; the criteria of systematic theology are analogous to hermeneutics, rhetoric, and poetics; the criteria of practical theology are analogous to ethics and politics. All these theological criteria are, of course, only analogous insofar as they must be transformed twice: first, by the postclassical exigencies of our historically and socially mediated modern situation; and, second, transformed yet anew by the exigencies of the explicitly Christian center of gravity proper to Christian theology. Yet these classic extra theological criteria remain genuinely analogous to those employed in a public theology. If heeded to, they might free us all to recognize that theology functions as a critically collaborative enterprise open to all who honor comprehensive notions of both reason and praxis.

NOTES

1. The most helpful general studies here remain Nicholas Lobkowicz, *Theory and Practice: History of a Concept from Aristotle to Marx* (Notre Dame: University of Notre Dame Press, 1969); and Richard Bernstein, *Praxis and Action* (Philadelphia: University of Pennsylvania Press, 1971).
2. I have tried to defend the major claims of the following two sections on "fundamental" and "systematic" theology in two books: *Blessed Rage for Order: The New Pluralism in Theology* (New York: Seabury, 1975) and *The Analogical Imagination: Christian Theology and the Culture of Pluralism* (New York: Crossroad Books, 1981). For an abbreviated version of these two "subdisciplines" in theology, see *The Analogical Imagination,* pp. 47–99. The necessary documentation for the categories and the literature surrounding their discussion may be found in those two volumes.
3. For this phrase, see the discussions in *Consensus in Theology? A Dialogue with Hans Küng and Edward Schillebeeckx,* ed. Leonard Swidler (Philadelphia: Westminster, 1980).
4. See Hans-Georg Gadamer, *Truth and Method* (New York: Seabury, 1975). For Gadamer on "application," pp. 274–309; for my own comments on his position, see *The Analogical Imagination,* p. 90, n. 59, and pp. 135–36, n. 8.
5. The "more comprehensive" refer to postpositivist notions of reason. The literature here is immense; for a representative survey, see *Rationality Today; La Rationalité Aujourd'hui,* ed. Theodore F. Geratts (Ottawa: The University of Ottawa Press, 1979).

6. For the defense of this notion of the "classic," see *The Analogical Imagination,* p. 99–154.

7. See Paul Ricoeur, *Interpretation Theory* (Fort Worth: Texas Christian University Press, 1976).

8. The chief criterion, in my judgment, is whether the demands for the praxis of authentic *conversation* are allowed. Here, Gadamer's phenomenology of conversation remains central.

9. Besides the works of Lobkowicz and Bernstein referred to above, I have been informed here by the clear summary of Thomas McCarthy in *The Critical Theory of Jürgen Habermas* (Cambridge, Mass.: The MIT Press, 1978), pp. 1–16.

10. A helpful study here is Raymond Geuss, *The Idea of a Critical Theory: Habermas and the Frankfurt School* (Cambridge: Cambridge University Press, 1981).

11. I assume here the continued relevance of the concerns of "metaethics" as related to "metaphysics"—the proper concern of "fundamental" theology.

5. Dimensions of Practical Theology: Meaning, Action, Self

THOMAS W. OGLETREE

THE MOST difficult questions confronting theological education today concern our attempts to work out suitable relations between what we are wont to call academic and practical aspects of theological study.

There is widespread recognition that the isolation from each other of academic and practical studies in theological education results in an unsatisfactory state of affairs. When we allow these two interests to undergo separate development, we impoverish and distort them both. On the one hand, we tend to subject our academic activities almost exclusively to considerations internal to the unfolding logic of the subspecialities of theological study. The several disciplines then dominate the direction of thought and inquiry rather than serve as resources for engaging the pressing questions of human existence. We lose a sense of connection between critical thought and vital life concerns. On the other hand, we tend in our practical thinking to become preoccupied with technique. We learn to perfect "means" to accomplish specific practical "ends" without considering the wider ramifications of either. The techniques in question may consist in conventional "recipe knowledge,"[1] quite specific procedures for handling this or that problem. More likely, they are borrowed without criticism or adaptation from secular frames of reference: management, psychotherapy, communications, education. In either case distinctively theological understandings are displaced by unexamined assumptions and premises. Ironically, both the abstraction of academic undertakings from life realities and the

reduction of practical knowledge to technique conspire to con-
firm and reinforce the dominant patterns of an existing world,
transforming theological substance into ideology.

Recognizing the hiatus between academic and practical studies, our first impulse may be simply to build some bridges, to
establish some connections. The task, it seems, is to devise ways
of integrating modes of thought that have gotten separated from
each other. Thus, we encourage the academically oriented to
venture some practical life applications of the knowledge they
have gained; and we urge the practically minded to draw more
widely on the resources of the academic disciplines in "reflecting" on the meaning of concrete human involvements. We hope
for some mutual enrichment of the two activities, perhaps a
fuller realization of the elemental unity of thought and practical
experience.

Such ad hoc responses can scarcely suffice, however, for they
are unable to address the deeper problems that underlie our
manifest difficulties. What we need is a reconstruction of our
understandings of the relation of theory and practice in our theological work, and of the distinctions and connections between
theoretical and practical knowledge that figure in that relation.
Such a reconstruction might permit us to examine critically our
existing theological disciplines and assess their appropriateness
for theological study. Yet it probably should not, indeed, could
not, simply displace these disciplines. Too much has already
been gained by their development and employment, both in
terms of critical method and of specialized bodies of knowledge.
What we primarily gain is a means of placing the contributions
of the disciplines in a frame of reference more suited to the practice of faith at which theology aims. By the same token, the
needed reconstruction cannot merely stand in opposition to technique. Effective practice involves technical knowledge and the
skills to use it appropriately. What we seek is a broader and
richer sense of practice, one that permits us to specify and delim-
it the role technique plays in our worldly involvements.

My aim in this chapter is to contribute to a reconstruction of
the principal features of theological study in their relation to one
another. The guiding thesis is that all theology, properly con-

ceived, is practical theology, certainly where the education of ministers is in view. Thus, practical theology is not one of the branches of theology; the term practical rather characterizes the central intent of theology treated as a whole. Where distinctions are made among discrete theological tasks, it is better to speak of dimensions of practical theology, not of practical theology in opposition, let us say, to historical theology or philosophical theology.

Theology is practical in the sense that it concerns, in all of its expressions, the most basic issues of human existence. It has to do with the human pilgrimage in its totality: with its meaning and significance, with the determination of appropriate responses to the realities we confront during its course, with the growth of persons in community, with the construction of institutions suited to human well-being. The origin of theology is practical; it arises out of prior worldly involvements. Its end is likewise practical; it plunges us once more into the sea of experience. If our deliberations as theologians are sound, then we learn to immerse ourselves with deeper insight, understanding, and fidelity in those worldly realities that make up our lives. We apprehend anew and with greater wisdom and maturity what was in no small measure already ours. Whenever and wherever we take it up, theology is bound up with the practical rhythms of human life.

Theology does have a theoretical side. Yet the theoretical does not stand in opposition to practical knowledge. It arises as a moment within practical theology itself, a moment in which, relatively speaking, we distance ourselves from the immediacies of experience. We distance ourselves from experience in order to see more clearly what is given to us, or what is going on around us or in us. The seeing is not an end in itself. It is a movement that permits us to incorporate the various facets of experience more fully into our knowing, doing, and being. The possibility of objectifying what is given to experience is a peculiarity of self-consciousness, our power not only to relate to our world consciously, but to do so with a consciousness of the manner of relating itself. A theoretical orientation is not intrinsically opposed to practicality; it is an attitude we take up for quite practical reasons. If we separate the theoretical stance from all practical interests and obscure its rootage in a broader life matrix, we distort it and risk deceiving ourselves about the nature of our thought processes.

Since theoretical studies are themselves practical in import, it is better to speak of them not as a self-contained type of inquiry, but as a movement of distancing within practical undertakings. They belong to an ongoing rhythm of distancing and immersion in human knowing, doing, and being. By using such language, we correct the tendencies of modern thought to conceive dichotomies where polar tensions and dialectical interactions are in view. We challenge, for example, the all too common split in understanding between the theoretical and the practical, the objective and the subjective, fact and value. When we fall victim to such dichotomies, we tend as well to depreciate the latter terms of these pairs to a lower status in human understanding: *mere* practical application, *mere* subjectivity, *mere* value preferences. The aim is to grasp their role in the dynamics of human understanding.

In what follows I will identify and describe three dimensions of practical theology: a meaning dimension, an action dimension, and a self dimension. Action will be examined in its institutional setting, and selfhood will be associated with the communal relations that constitute it. These three dimensions are essential to an adequate account of practical theology. When we are dealing with education for ministry, we must, therefore, be attentive in some fashion to them all. In referring to each of these dimensions, I will indicate a range of relevant theoretical studies. In order to further the specific practical interests involved, we undertake a distancing movement. But the distancing movement is not an end in itself; it remains dialectically related to our continual reimmersion in the ongoing rhythms of life.

Finally, I will suggest, the primary integrative problems in theological education do not revolve around efforts to incorporate particular theoretical insights into their corresponding practical interests. This task proves to be not so difficult when we keep in view the rootage of the theoretical stance in our practical life involvements. The more troublesome integrative problems concern the interrelations of the dimensions of practical theology, especially once each has been given relatively independent development. The problem is to bring together into a significant unity our thinking and our acting and our being. Here, of course, we confront not simply methodological or pedagogical or even therapeutic considerations. We also confront the fundamental brokenness of human being, our persistent implication in evil. Reflections on theological education cannot skirt the awful reality of human sinfulness.

Dimensions of Practical Theology

The Meaning Dimension

What I am calling the meaning dimension of practical theology concerns our ways of articulating and interpreting the understandings of our worldly being that are given us in faith. These understandings are borne in no small measure by the traditions we have received and in turn pass along to oncoming generations. Attending to the traditions we share involves us with texts and the processes of their interpretation.

For the meaning dimension, the central interest is in truth. The truth at issue is not one that can be delivered simply by the correct application of the proper methods. It is not, that is to say, the outcome of carefully pursued theoretical studies, though there is a limited and secondary sense of truth appropriate to such studies. The truth that is here at stake concerns a disclosure of the meaning of being and our placement in it. Such truth has a revelatory quality to it, the sense that something previously hidden from view has been uncovered, brought out of concealment. This disclosure communicates to us how little we have a direct and uncomplicated interest in the truth. In fact, we love darkness rather than light because our deeds are evil. We are, as Søren Kierkegaard put it, in a polemical relation to the truth.[2] Nonetheless, it is the truth and only the truth that sets us free. Such truth is clearly not fundamentally theoretical; it is through and through practical. Its discernment continually coalesces with the occurrence of redemption.

Our interest in apprehending and articulating the truth calls forth theoretical studies. It embraces a moment of distancing. The distancing represents our self-conscious effort to establish at least a partial corrective to our tendencies to distort and obscure the truth. It is occasioned by at least three considerations. First, the traditions that attest the truth for us have been sedimented in texts. Insofar as we have an interest in allowing these texts to speak to us, to teach us something we do not already know, we have need of distancing procedures that will allow the texts to show themselves as they are. We seek methodological checks against our tendencies to project our own distorted understandings upon the texts. Thus, we develop and utilize historical and literary methods for reading those texts and assessing their significance. Yet the readings gained through such distancing are not ends in themselves. They are oriented toward our own practical apprehension of the truth that comes to expression in the texts. We seek, therefore, to appropriate what is said in the texts, or better, to assimilate our lives to the realities they uncover for us. Such texts can be said to speak the truth insofar as that which they utter genuinely becomes our truth as well.

When we seek to appropriate into our own meaning-worlds what is offered in the texts, we have need of a second set of theoretical operations. This set has to do with our attempts to relate coherently the truth given to faith to the rest of our critically interpreted experience. Here we seek to resist a bifurcation of experience—belonging to the first century in our piety (or seeming to!) and to the twentieth century in our secular lives.

The task confronting us here is by no means a small one, for the dominant modes of thought in modern societies do not easily allow for the sense of truth that is vital to the life of faith. We are faced with the necessity of providing an account of human understanding that displays not simply the possibility, but the primacy of a faith stance in the human manner of being in the world. Consequently, some theologians take up philosophical inquiries—often of a rather esoteric sort and with the aid of a strange technical language—for the sake of clarifying the nature and status in human experience of those realities given to faith. For persons interested in theological education to belittle or perhaps bypass such undertakings is not, despite appearances, a very practical thing to do. The practice of faith depends profoundly on a sense of truth. When that sense of truth is weakened or undermined, then we are in danger as well of losing the substance of ministry. Nonetheless, the theoretical moves accomplished by way of philosophical inquiries are not ends in themselves. Cogency of argument is never sufficient where faith is concerned. Analyses and arguments and rigorous descriptions must give way to an elemental recognition and acknowledgment of the liberating truth given to faith. Their end is a "second naiveté" (to borrow a term from Paul Ricoeur) in which we present ourselves as children before the Holy One.[3]

Finally, when we take up the fuller articulation of the meaning of faith, we become involved in the thematic development of its contents. We seek to offer the clearest, most precise and coherent account of those themes that we can manage, though without reducing them to categories wholly at our disposal. Here too distancing is involved. We subject ourselves to the demands of linguistic comprehensibility. We take on the disciplines of clarity, logical consistency, and conceptual coherence in setting forth constructively the truths we apprehend. We look to the great teachers of the church to assist us in carrying out this task.

Here too the theoretical moment is not an end in itself. The truth given to faith does not and cannot reside in a set of categories, no matter how clear and distinct. We take up this distancing stance because of our attempt to grasp with fidelity the central thrust of the truth that has been delivered to us. We seek to resist mixing that truth with notions alien to it, perhaps finally incompatible with it. This quest for fidelity cannot, of course, be accomplished by the mere repetition of well-established conventions of thought. Such a strategy ossifies the truth of faith and so removes it from us as a living reality. Rather in each generation we venture fresh articulations of the content of faith. In the process we engage our total culture anew, risking those distortions we call heresies, that the explosive power of the truth we honor might find its way once more into language. These ventures, moreover, cannot come to rest simply in "thought experiments," even though we continually undertake such experiments on a provisional basis. They finally concern understandings upon which we are prepared to stake our lives. Attention to this dimension of theology could scarcely be more profoundly practical.

To sum up, the meaning dimension of theology concerns the mediation and appropriation of those traditions that bear to us the meaning of being and our placement in it. The practical interest is in truth, a truth upon which we will stake our lives. The relevant theoretical moments of this dimension are directed toward the critical accomplishment of the appropriation that is in view. Because it deals with the interpretation of texts and the thematic development of their contents, this dimension may be the one most easily addressed in a traditional classroom setting, provided its link with elemental life involvements is not obscured. However, this dimension is not only distinct from the others; it is also essentially interrelated with them. Consequently, it too can receive adequate attention only if the peculiar dynamics of the other dimensions are fully in play. In fact, for many persons the issues residing in the meaning dimension of theological education can themselves come into focus only by way of one or both of the others.

The Action Dimension

The action dimension concerns our ways of enacting Christian faith in the building up of the church and in the implementation of its mission to the world. Here we have to do with sensibly manifest body movements: movements to produce the means of our subsistence as organic beings, to construct those objects that mark a distinctively human world—tools, works of art, houses, temples. Above all, we have to do with those facial expressions, gestures, sounds, touches, caresses—in some cases, physical assaults—that are the stuff of human interactions.

The meaning dimension provides a horizon of intelligibility for the action dimension; but it does not in itself wholly encompass or control that dimension. Action brings something new into play; it does not merely apply meanings. In fact, it establishes and maintains the life contexts that are essential to the appearance of any humanly significant meanings. In this respect it profoundly conditions the meanings we are able to entertain in the course of our lives.

In the action dimension we find much that is routinized. Indeed, if most of us did not for the most part act in highly typical ways, a human world would not be possible at all. These routinized ways of acting are in many cases role related. Education for ministry includes considerable attention to institutionalized expectations of what ministers are to do. There are ritual actions that enable communities of faith to reenact in a social drama their sense of who they are and what they are about. There are acts of caring directed toward those who suffer. There is instruction for the young, for the novices, and perhaps, for the edification of the saints. Routinized actions establish, maintain, and build up the continuity of life within communities of faith, indeed, within the whole of human society.

Other actions are strategic. They consist in particular responses to particular situations. They require fresh judgments about what is to be done, for example, to maintain the health and vitality of the community and to engage the world in mission.

For the action dimension, the central interest is in appropriateness. One seeks to discern what is right and proper to do in specific situations. Appropriateness is not simply a moral category. Ritual actions, for example, call forth aesthetic judgments, as do attempts to produce works of art that articulate faith understandings in a nonverbal fashion. The sermon itself is not simply cognitive in nature; it too is an aesthetic production, one, moreover, with prominent ritual elements. And appropriateness certainly points toward a fit in action with the truth disclosed to faith. The meaning horizon of faith is always a factor in judgments of appropriateness.

Even so, where action is in view, moral considerations loom large, especially when we are subjecting routinized actions to critical scrutiny, or seeking to respond with prophetic insight to the worldly realities we confront, both inside and outside of the church. Here we seek material norms to guide us: notions of love and justice. We seek ways to give concrete expression to those norms in the typical situations we confront.

Action does not simply involve judgments of appropriateness. It also presupposes and mobilizes skills and competencies, the ability to carry out what one has judged to be fitting, to insert one's projects into the ongoing course of worldly happenings. Indeed, action involves courage and self-control as well, but these motifs already point us toward that third dimension of practical theology, the self dimension. Of course, the interpretative tasks associated with the meaning dimension also call for skills. But these skills can be developed and evaluated in the relatively safe environment of a school setting, where concrete engagement in ministry has been provisionally suspended, or perhaps not yet taken up in practice. They enter directly into the action dimension only when they are enacted in settings where ministry is going on. To attend to the action dimension within theological education, therefore, some sort of field education is necessary. Here persons try themselves out in actual situations of ministry. With the help of supervisors and peer associates, they learn to reflect critically on their accomplishments. They learn to improve the quality of their judgments and actions by subjecting their experiences to review.

Here too there are theoretical moments, indeed, quite a range of them. To begin with, we seek to distance ourselves from our taken-for-granted, conventional notions of appropriateness. We want to see if these notions stand up under careful scrutiny. For this distancing, historical studies, including work with authoritative texts, plays an important role. Now, however, the accent falls not simply on the reading of formative texts, or on the ways in which the great teachers of the church have interpreted those texts; it falls as well on how leaders within the church have sought to give suitable organizational form to Christian communities, and how they have negotiated the relationships of these communities with other organizational and institutional expressions of human social existence—the family, the state, the economic order, and so on. This distancing movement enables us to see more clearly how organizational and institutional forms shape our discernment of appropriateness. It alerts us to the ways in which these forms influence or even determine the actions that are likely to emerge as realistic possibilities, ruling others out of consideration or rendering them ineffectual from the outset. We gain a profound awareness that enactment involves not simply the treasures given to us in faith, but also the earthen vessels bearing them. We learn that the latter, moreover, are not mere containers. They are constitutive features in the actual living out of what is understood.

The human sciences facilitate a distancing from our concrete worldly engagements. Studies in developmental psychology, social psychology, the sociology of organizational behavior, the sociology of religion, and political economy provide us with a new angle of vision on our quest for the appropriate enactment of Christian faith. They surface dynamics that constrain and channel our action possibilities. They suggest the sorts of skills and competencies likely to be requisite for effective action amid those realities making up our social existence. We discover, for example, that the church will function in modern secular societies as a voluntary association, however it may prefer to understand itself theologically. A general awareness of how voluntary associations work will, therefore, affect our perceptions of what is involved in the concrete enactment of ministry.

Under what conditions do such associations survive and fail? What permits them to flourish, to accomplish their goals? What causes them to flounder? Such considerations have practical importance for ministry.

Yet neither historical nor human science objectifications of the action dimension are ends in themselves. They cannot pronounce the final word, certainly not where practical theology is concerned. They are legitimate only insofar as they enable us provisionally to distance ourselves from our previous actions and from our ongoing action contexts. In particular they alert us to the constraints on action and to some of the conditions for effective action. Yet the practical interest remains paramount. It concerns the discernment of appropriate ways to enact Christian faith in concrete life settings.

There is a third sort of distancing within the action dimension that also deserves mention. It is a move that has become a crucial part of field education. It consists in the attempts of apprentice ministers to objectify their own performances, to "catch themselves" in the act of ministry. The relevant devices are verbatims, accounts of critical incidents, descriptions of settings of ministry, and so forth. The use of these devices, I would suggest, amounts to genuinely theoretical studies, even though such studies are much closer to concrete action than historical or human science investigations. Their connection with the search for appropriate and effective action is, as a result, much more manifest.

To sum up, the action dimension of practical theology concerns the concrete enactment of Christian faith in the ongoing course of worldly events. At issue are appropriateness and effectiveness. The relevant theoretical studies provide us with resources for reflecting on these matters and their crucial conditions. They also alert us to how we actually perform, in distinction from our unexamined notions about the meaning and import of our acts.

The Self Dimension

Practical theology finally concerns the formation of human selves. Here we have to do with the embodiment of Christian faith in the lives of persons. We have to do with those continuities and stabilities that make up our specific identities, orient us to the world in particular ways, and provide us with particular resources for acting—skills, competencies, virtues, excellencies of character.

The practical interest at stake in the self dimension, I would suggest, is fidelity. In speaking of the self and its maturation, we are sometimes inclined to identify the relevant normative standard as integrity or authenticity. Yet the treatment of these notions in modern thought is significantly marked by images of autonomy, which may not fit well with the central thrust of Christian faith. For the Christian life, the pressing issue is faith, embracing trust and obedience. Faith accents the fact that we do not contain our being within ourselves. That being rather lies outside ourselves in our relationships with others, other human beings, to be sure, but especially the Divine Other who is present to us as creative power, righteous judgment, unconditional grace, liberating promise. To keep in view the centrality of relationships for Christian understanding, I would speak of the practical interest of the self dimension as a concern for fidelity. Insofar as my life has integrity, that integrity resides in my fidelity to the cause that is also the source of my life, my being, and my worth.

In the self dimension of practical theology, the task in ministry is to create those contexts and to make those moves that encourage, call forth, and support fidelity. With this accent we are no longer concerned simply with individual selves; we are concerned with human communities, their formation and development, their growth and maturation. Fidelity involves persons in community with those who share a common heritage and a common cause. Such is the essential context for human growth. Such is, from another standpoint, the end of human growth. Faithful communities in the Christian tradition are oriented to the world. They exist in mission to the world. But they are never mere "means" to mission, instruments of emancipatory activity. They are also ends in themselves, the advance and representative embodiments of the unity and wholeness promised for all.

We know full well, however, that fidelity is in no sense a simple, straightforward accomplishment. In fact, it is not finally a human accomplishment at all, but a fruit of divine grace. In our actual existence, fidelity is continually being undermined and blocked—by our anxieties, our compulsions, by past injuries which have made us wary and self-protective, by oppressive social structures which warp and distort our beings. Infidelity characterizes us as much or more than fidelity, and the infidelity attests our bondage to psychic, social, and spiritual powers that in no small measure lie beyond our control. The possibility of fidelity rests upon our emancipation from bondage.

Insofar as we attend to the self dimension in theological education, the theological school itself is very much a part of the real world, not a place of retreat for the sake of growth in understanding. The theological school participates in the brokenness of society and confronts daily the principalities and powers that would rule that society. The theological school itself is made up of persons who suffer under various sorts of compulsions and bear the scars of deep hurts. We are in need of deliverance even as we seek to mediate the possibility of deliverance to others. Education for ministry cannot set aside or neglect the personal beings of those who are involved in it. It has an emancipatory task as a feature in its total work.

There is a theoretical moment in this emancipatory interest.

For one thing we have symbolic articulations in religious language of our bondage to evil, indeed, our active implication in it. These materials themselves objectify our experiences to some extent. They name it and interpret it. We also have at our disposal psychological and sociological accounts of human bondage relevant to our interest in the formation of selves. Through these accounts we discern the rootage of our compulsions in psychosocial dynamics, or in the class conflicts that manifest themselves in the systemic oppression of the many by those few who have gained dominance. Some of the most difficult questions confronting practical theology concern the relation between the psychic and social sources of human bondage, and Christian accounts of its deeper, religious basis. In light of these objectifying accounts of the sources of human bondage we have corresponding therapies and means of conscientization. We seek to relate their operations to the spiritual guidance that serves the embodiment of Christian faith in human life. All of these approaches objectify in some fashion the bases of our brokenness and the promise of our emancipation. They help us discern what is going on in our lives as we reach out for the fulfillment of our beings as persons in community. Yet these theoretical movements, these acts of distancing, always gain their significance from the role they play in the growth and maturation of persons in the Christian life. They concern the formation of faithful lives and faithful communities.

The self dimension of practical theology requires us to incorporate into theological education attention to the formation of persons. Of course, students who take up theological studies are already in large measure "formed." The aim is to help them assimilate more fully what has already taken place in their lives, and to develop disciplines and life practices relevant to their continuing growth. It involves supporting and encouraging their attempts to work through hurts that are personally disabling, to gain insight into anxieties and fears that blunt their effectiveness, to discern and accept limits that give legitimate shape and direction to their concrete life commitments. Moves of a theoretical sort, distancing moves, are essential to these processes. Perhaps students take up the discipline of writing a spiritual autobiography and talking it through with peers or educational guides. Perhaps they seek out a spiritual director who assists them in getting in touch with life possibilities that prayer and meditation can open up. Perhaps they commit themselves to regular corporate worship, self-consciously testing their quest for a suitable piety against historic liturgical traditions. Perhaps they place themselves in a therapeutic context that permits them to relearn some basic life patterns. In each instance one distances oneself from what is going on in one's own personal experiencing in order to grow in a fidelity that is the promise of selfhood. Where the rhythms of distancing and incorporation become a part of the life of a self, that self is in a position to take responsibility for his or her ongoing development as a human being.

Thus, we have three dimensions of practical theology. We have a meaning dimension in which we seek to appropriate the truth borne by our traditions into our own meaning worlds; we have an action dimension in which we seek to enact in the ongoing course of worldly events those projects that correspond to our sense of what is right and fitting; and we have a self dimension in which we seek to embody in our own beings and to enable in the beings of others that fidelity which is the telos of Christian existence. Each of these dimensions has its distinctive practical interests; each has its corresponding forms of distancing that in the rhythm of life serve and promote those interests. In all cases the practical interests provide the grounds and the reasons for the distancing moves. The theoretical studies are but way stations leading to the appropriation of truth, the enactment of the fitting, and the embodiment of the two in faithful lives.

Integrating the Dimensions of Practical Theology

What can we now say about integration? The principal integrative problems in practical theology, I am contending, have to do with the relations among the dimensions of practical theology, not the incorporation of various kinds of theoretical studies into their corresponding practical interests. The task is to realize a measure of unity in our knowing, doing, and being. Not surprisingly, the integration that accomplishes the overall interest of practical theology is indistinguishable from that which constitutes the promise of Christian life. It is through and through an eschatological hope, though we may fragmentarily enjoy its first fruits in the midst of our earthly pilgrimage. When the problem is stated in these terms, we remind ourselves that the integration that concerns us is not fundamentally a methodological or pedagogical problem. It is an existential matter, with all the complexities and ambiguities that suggests.

We cannot deal adequately with theological education if we do not keep these existential considerations in view. In fact, they provide us with organizing principles for dealing with methodological and pedagogical issues. Even so, I want to bring to the fore the methodological and pedagogical issues since these are the ones for which we can most directly assume responsibility. I want to look at them in light of the origin and end of our interest in integration, and especially of its fragmentary realizations "in the middle."

With reference to the origins, there is, I would suggest, a pre-reflective unity of experience out of which the specifiable dimensions of practical theology emerge. This unity is based in the fact that we learn to know what our world is like and how to act in it appropriately at the same time as we begin to gain some centering in our being as selves. Knowing, doing, and being are by no means essentially separated or opposed. Essentially, they belong together, constantly interpenetrating, conditioning, and shaping one another. At the same time, the complexity of human existence is such that strains inevitably appear in the relations of the three, strains leading to fractures, dichotomies. What we do is never a simple expression of who we are, especially, for example, when our social roles are at odds with our personal sense of self. Likewise, what we self-consciously think we understand, value, and hold to be appropriate may be out of phase with our actual deeds and our concrete identities as selves. Within each of these three life dimensions, contradictions continually emerge, disclosing the brokenness of our being. Just as the bases of integration in practical theology are already present in lived experience, so also are the barriers to such integration. I would suggest further that the barriers derive their power from the positive bases. The barriers are distorted expressions of the more fundamental drive toward the unity of experience. Accomplishing integration concretely involves activating these primordial bases of unity and breaking through or overcoming the barriers.

Despite the elemental yet complex unity of experience, the process of examining with care its constituent features leads to differentiations. Here methodological considerations do become significant, especially when we seek—as I think we should—to take advantage of the gains in understanding promised by theoretical studies. We cannot simultaneously focus our attention on the linguistic expressions that articulate our sense of a meaningful world,.on the patterns within human interactions that make up our social life, and on the dynamics by which we are formed as selves. The focusing necessarily brings some aspects of experience into relief and pushes others into the background. It abstracts and isolates these aspects from the totality of experience. Since the methods that allow us to accomplish this focusing point in somewhat different directions, we find ourselves tending toward a certain fragmentation of experience in our thinking. This fragmentation is not simply a result of an inevitable human faultedness; it is in no small measure a function of specialization in our disciplined inquiries. It is fragmentation of the latter kind that we are particularly obliged to overcome in theological education, even while not ignoring its deeper existential basis.

How shall we take up this challenge? The principal point I would make is that the integration we seek cannot be accomplished in a specific sector of the curriculum, let us say, in systematic theology, or in a reflection group associated with field education. Either it is a function of the movement of the total curriculum, the total educational experience, or it cannot occur in a fashion that does justice to all essential dimensions of practical theology. This observation suggests that the crucial integrative problems in theological education cannot be solved by the introduction of special, integrative courses, nor even by a well-designed curriculum. In considerable measure it requires a community of scholars and teachers with diverse competencies who have learned to respect one another and to engage one another seriously in an ongoing discourse about theological education. Successful curricular development rests upon effective faculty development. A faculty made up of persons who have come to understand and value the contributions of colleagues to a total undertaking will be in a position to suggest and develop relations among the dimensions of practical theology at many points in the movement of a program of studies. Given the highly competitive and individualistic character of much higher education, this goal cannot be easily realized. Nonetheless, it deserves no small amount of our attention and energy.

Having pointed to the total curriculum and the total educational experience as the proper context for integration in practical theology, there is yet need, I believe, for particular settings, particular educational experiences, where the integration of knowing, doing, and being is the explicit theme and the paramount task. Even in these settings, which probably have to come relatively late in a program of studies, one cannot presume to provide students with all they require for a unified experience. Rather, the aim must be to help them draw in appropriate ways on all of their learnings, testing themselves out in a critical and supportive communal setting. Ideally, such settings will be important for continuing faculty growth as well.

In these processes we seek the reintegration of experience, but now on a higher, more critical level of awareness and with a fuller mobilization of our powers of being. We seek above all a more mature understanding of the complexity of life, and hence, a determination to resist simplistic solutions that unify experience only by truncating it, by closing out some of its crucial aspects. Insofar as such accomplishments take place in the process of theological education, they will, of course, only be provisional; they are way stations, temporary resting places, in the larger movement of life.

If teachers do their work well, their students will come to appreciate at a deep level that the integration to which practical theology points calls for lifelong learning and is finally an eschatological hope. They will take up their ministries with a readiness to struggle on an ongoing basis with these issues, continually deepening the level at which they reach out for wholeness and fullness of being. Struggling with fidelity, we may dare to hope and to trust that the high prize promised to us all will in actuality become ours.

NOTES

1. The analogy of recipes to characterize everyday knowledge is taken from Alfred Schutz, *Collected Papers,* Vol. I, *The Problem of Social Reality,* ed. with introduction by Maurice Natanson (The Hague: Martinus Nijhoff, 1967), pp. 19, 21.
2. *Philosophical Fragments or A Fragment of Philosophy,* trans. with introduction and notes by David F. Swenson (Princeton: Princeton University Press, 1956), pp. 39–43. Originally published under the pseudonym Johannes Climacus.
3. Paul Ricoeur, *The Symbolism of Evil,* trans. Emerson Buchanan (Boston: Beacon Press, 1967), p. 351.

III

SOME REGIONS OF
PRACTICAL THEOLOGY

6. Practical Theology and Social Action: Or What Can the 1980s Learn from the 1960s?

DENNIS P. McCANN

I HAVE chosen to approach this topic in light of my own experience in the 1960s as a social activist seminarian, because the problems then encountered initially led me to read, among other things, the Latin American theologies of liberation and to reflect on their relevance to what I'd done and thought. After four years of reading and reflecting at the Divinity School of the University of Chicago, I gained enough credits to pass myself off as an academic, but somewhere along the way I became increasingly disenchanted with these theologies. So much so that in my recent book, *Christian Realism and Liberation Theology*,[1] I argue that they do not provide a promising model for practical theology. The reasons given there aspire to be rigorously theoretical. They involve the nature of religious experience and the tasks of theology. They appeal to a theory of religious "limit-situations" and theological "limit-concepts" for warrants—in short, just the sort of thing you'd expect from an "academic" theologian. What is not made clear there is how practical these reasons are. Since I remain convinced that the fate of practical theology in North America in the 1980s will depend on how well we respond to the challenge of these and similar theologies, here I will try to show what it was about my practical experience in the 1960s that inspired my all-too-theoretical reflections. The results may strike many as rather old hat. They are meant to be.

A Social Activist's Crisis

I began my brief career as a social activist in the summer of 1965 in Columbus, Ohio. A number of us Catholic seminarians—I was a college sophomore at the time, and it showed—became involved with Lutheran and Presbyterian students in what was known locally as the "Ecumenical Inner-City Project." Besides doing the usual good deeds like helping poor blacks paint and fix up their homes or running vacation Bible schools for their children, we were also involved in a "grass roots" organizing campaign. We were hoping to form an interlocking set of neighborhood councils to give the "ghetto" greater political visibility. By day we would canvass the neighborhoods on such issues as the quality of basic city services—street lights and sewer repair, garbage collection, police and fire protection, and the deteriorating condition of the neighborhood schools—in the hope of showing people the connection between their complaints and their lack of political power. By night, beside attending one interminable meeting after another, we were reading and discussing the theory of community organization as told by Saul Alinsky and Nicholas von Hoffmann. The more intellectually adventuresome among us were also reading Harvey Cox's *The Secular City,* as we tried to discover the possible theological implications of what we were up to.

Within a few weeks or so things had begun to take off. Given the way the world works, none of us viewed our modest efforts on Columbus's near east side apart from larger events happening elsewhere. We identified ourselves and were identified with Martin Luther King's "dream" and the March on Washington, with the too-good-to-be-true image of Lyndon Johnson singing "We Shall Overcome," and with the activities of the "kids from SNCC" across the South. It is hard to pinpoint exactly when it happened, but some of us began to be radicalized. Sooner or later those of us who were realized that the moderately reformist strategies of our inner-city project would have to be criticized in a way not previously anticipated. And being an impressionable youth, I was all for it.

Nor was this transformation merely political. That summer of my twentieth year was the first time I had been let loose in a relatively unstructured environment. Prior to that, it had been mostly either the "monastery"—as my sister once lovingly characterized our strict Irish-Catholic home—or the seminary. Without having much insight into the way in which it was happening, that summer I got "liberated." The details are unimportant; what is important is its impact on my religious life. What had been plausible and effective in the seminary—the daily regimen of prayer and meditation geared to the rhythms of the Catholic liturgical year—just seemed irrelevant in the streets. Not only did we simply not have time for organized spiritual exercises, but there appeared to be no need for them, given our new experience of Christ in our poor black neighbor. Even so, there were some moments when I had misgivings about my own liberation.

I remember one midsummer's night when just the Catholic seminarians got together. We were on the back porch of the rectory when our clerical benefactor treated us to a case or two of beer. Before we could get it opened, one of the deacons said, "Hey, what about compline?" How long had it been since we had gathered as Catholic seminarians at prayer? Without putting too fine a point on it, he whipped out his brand new breviary and there on the back porch, surrounded by the sounds of summer in the city, we lifted our voices to the chants of the church. With noticeable fervor, too. Afterward, as we broke open the beer, some of us tried to put into words the deeper meaning of this episode. On that night, at least, it still seemed possible to reconcile the old ways with a new spirit.

What began that summer continued on for the next two years, as our group made its contribution to the rise and fall of the Great Society. Its centerpiece, President Johnson's War on Poverty, called for "maximum feasible participation of the poor" in the political decisions that affect them. We responded by organizing a city-wide coalition of inner-city churches, independent settlement houses, and civil rights organizations. The Peoples Poverty Board, as it came to be named, had a brief run, but in that time it was linked with most of the "urban unrest" that people downtown imagined was going on in Columbus. When we organized a statewide "Poor Peoples Conference" and brought in

SCLC's Andrew Young to speak, we were accused of importing "outside agitators." When we picketed the police station to protest the savage beating of a black Baptist clergyman, we were all meticulously photographed and catalogued by the antisubversive squad. When Detroit and Newark blew up the next summer, city officials became convinced that we were planning something similar for Columbus. Yet despite this atmosphere of increasing paranoia—or better, because of it—we continued our organizing efforts, though without much lasting success. That harmless "summer apostolate," in short, had led me to a deeply personal identification with the political struggle of the ghetto's militant minority.

This transformation, inevitably, had its effect on my religious life. The camaraderie of the back porch had collapsed when subjected to the pressures of radical politics. Those of us who stayed with it were, spiritually, on our own. While some were able to make do with tracts for the times like Malcolm Boyd's *Are You Running with Me, Jesus?* I went through a kind of religious schizophrenia in which I became one sort of person in the seminary and another on the streets. While I yearned to break out of my spiritual isolation, I now felt that if Christ's presence was elusive in the prayer life of the church, it was no less ambiguous in a radical's identification with movements for liberation.

This troubling insight was crystallized for me at the National Conference for New Politics, held in Chicago during the late summer of 1967. While the conference was designed to unite the whole spectrum of social protest movements into a new national party, what actually occurred there made any coalition on the Left impossible. The point is not to reopen the political quarrels that marred that gathering. What struck me then as now was the way in which they were handled. Real discussion became impossible. The only thing that counted was who was more militant than whom, or who had proper credentials to speak for the world's oppressed. The level of political paranoia and moral chaos was as extreme as anything I've ever witnessed, either before or since. It turned into one more skirmish in the politics of confrontation. Only this time the passions aroused were to be directed against competing factions within the movement itself. Perhaps we'll never know how much of this was the work of government provocateurs, but the New Left emerged not strengthened but exhausted and in disarray. Or was it just my own sense of confusion and apprehension regarding the future? Either way, in a moment of complete demoralization I felt confronted with the utter ambiguity of all I'd thought and done in the previous three years. And I don't recall finding the spiritual resources—from either the seminary or the streets—to cope with that glimpse into the abyss.

Agenda for Practical Theology

Over the years since then it has slowly dawned on me that there is an agenda for practical theology hidden in the very ambivalence of my experience. Gradually I realized that in cases like mine there are two demons that prey upon Christian social activists—namely, excessive spiritualization and politicization.[2] Each evades the demands of Christian witness in the world, but in opposite ways. Both react against anxieties inevitably triggered by the ambiguous reality of social action: "excessive spiritualization," by exchanging ambiguity for the certainties of a conventional religious righteousness—like the rich young man who went away empty when Jesus commanded him to sell all and give to the poor (Mark 10:17–31); "politicization," by doing the same with an unconventional political righteousness—like the disciple who, when the woman anointed Jesus with oil of nard, protested that the perfume might have been sold and the money given to these same poor (Mark 14:3–9).[3] Both of these evasions appear in my own case. For not only was I drifting spiritually in a way that risked confusing Christian faith with the aspirations of the militants with whom I identified; but also in later trying to compensate for this drift, I risked using the faith as a crutch—more precisely, like the one who went away empty, I retired to the pious study of theology when faced with the demands of social action. For all that, it may be easier to name these demons than to exorcise them. They have been conjured up more than once in the polemics of theologians speaking as partisans for either the Left or the Right. But since I harbored both of them, I seek a practical theology that will help overcome both of them. How might it proceed to do so?

First, practical theology must focus just as clearly on sustaining a commitment to Christian social action as on initiating one. It is not enough simply to goad Christians into action. To put it in the idiom of liberation theology, preaching "solidarity with the oppressed" at best is only half of what's needed. For such solidarity will open up new possibilities not only for experiencing Christ in our neighbor and ourselves, but also for recognizing the Sin of the World in our neighbor and ourselves. Pious platitudes regarding the spiritual risks involved in social activism may be true as far as they go, but they cannot substitute for critical reflection seeking to identify and evaluate these risks in terms of the religious faith that motivated the commitment in the first place.

Second, for any practical theology to take on this task it must emerge from genuine dialogue with Christians already involved in social action. To speak once more in the idiom of liberation theology, it must respond to the needs of "basic communities" (*communidades de base*). Yet if this dialogue is to be genuine, it must amount to more than a theological carte blanche underwriting the aspirations of these communities. Granted, practical theology must mediate between the "basic communities" and the "mainstream" of the church by confronting the latter with the Christian witness of the former, but it must also mediate by confronting the former with the authentic traditions of the latter. Genuine dialogue, in short, must seek to initiate and sustain structures of mutual accountability between them both. Otherwise, Christian social activists are likely to become spiritually isolated and vulnerable to the twin demons that I encountered.

I will flesh out this agenda by comparing two models of practical theology, both of which respond to the problem dramatized in the first part of this chapter but do so in significantly different ways. The first of these models is based on Latin American liberation theology, especially as developed in the works of Gustavo Gutierrez and Juan Luis Segundo. I will label it "the 'orthopraxis' approach." The second is based on the Christian realism once popular with the World Council of Churches, especially as developed in the works of J. H. Oldham and John C. Bennett. I will label it "the 'middle-axioms' approach." I will argue that the latter addresses the problem of Christian social activism far better than the former; and I will try to show the reasons why.

Model A: Orthopraxis

Latin American liberation theology seems to provide a perfect answer to the questions I've raised. For not only does it show how "solidarity with the oppressed" is demanded by "the liberating God" of the Bible, but it also suggests how the demands of such solidarity may be met by participating in "basic communities" dedicated to the struggle for liberation. Liberation theology's reading of the Bible "in a revolutionary situation" thus provides both the outlines of a Christian spirituality adequate to the demands of social action and structures of Christian community in which that spirituality can flourish. At any rate, such is its promise on first reading.

Questions arise, however, on second reading regarding its capacity to sustain a Christian identity for either the individual social activist or the "basic communities." Does it, in short, check the tendency toward "excessive spiritualization" only by promoting the "politicization" of Christian faith? This suspicion can best be tested by asking what precisely liberation theologians mean by "critical reflection on praxis," for the distinctive claims of the "orthopraxis" approach derive from what's contained in this slogan.

While Gutierrez's initial formulation is innocent enough, the questionable implications of this program become clear as he develops it further. He begins by contrasting it with traditional notions of theology as "wisdom" and "rational knowledge" and describes "praxis" in terms of Christian love of neighbor.[4] "Critical reflection on praxis," then, refers initially to a theology seeking to emphasize the priority of love of neighbor for Christian social action. Nevertheless, when Gutierrez wants to be more specific, he speaks of "orthopraxis."[5] This concept—literally, "the right sort of praxis"—refers to the concrete struggles of "basic communities" seeking to give Christian witness in a revolutionary situation. While it does not necessarily involve "counter-violence" against "oppressors,"[6] whatever form it takes must be based on the communities' prior commitment to "liberation." Seen in this light, "critical reflection on praxis" thus redefines practical theology as the critical theory of Christians engaged in "orthopraxis."

But what is achieved by this redefinition? Why can't the same point be made by continuing to speak of the concrete demands of Christian love? The fact is that "orthopraxis" differs from love of neighbor precisely in its theory-ladenness. The "revolutionary situation" in which the basic communities operate is understood as such, thanks to the Marxist mode of analysis that defines the nature and tasks of "praxis."[7] So, in order to understand the significance of "orthopraxis," we must first get some idea of what Marxists mean by "praxis."

Two distinct uses of the term appear in Marxist analyses: one, descriptive; the other, normative.[8] In the first, "praxis" designates the fact that the human world is a social construction and not a reflection of the givenness of things, that it is the product of socially organized labor. Here "praxis" refers to our historic awareness of the difference between "nature" and "culture." In the second, "praxis" symbolizes the hope (or "historic necessity") that the dynamics of socially organized labor will lead to revolution or the full humanization of our world. Here "praxis" designates a vision of the substantive meaning of history as a whole, in terms of which Marxist analyses see the difference between "oppression" and "liberation." What is interesting about "praxis" is that these two uses are rarely, if ever, distinguished.[9] As a result, the meaning of "praxis" is frequently overdetermined, in the sense that it behaves like an "is" that thinks it's an "ought." In other words, what in one sense represents nothing more than the common presupposition of virtually all modern social theories, in another sense represents a substantive norm for criticizing them all. It is important to note that the "ought" in this case is no more entailed by the "is" than in any other similar theory.[10] Consequently, this anomaly in the Marxist concept of "praxis" is crucial for understanding the danger of "politicization" implicit in liberation theology.

What exactly happens, in other words, when this concept becomes the basis for liberation theology's notion of "orthopraxis"? Just as "praxis" allows the Marxist mode of analysis to define itself as a critical theory of society and its ideologies, so an "orthopraxis" modeled upon it allows liberation theology to define itself as a critical theory of the church and its theologies.

Not that there isn't any need for such, but what happens here is
that "praxis"—with all its ambiguity—tends to become the *principle* of criticism. The Marxist mode of analysis, in other words,
becomes constitutive of the "hermeneutic circle" of practical
theologies modeled on "orthopraxis." How else are we to understand Gutierrez when he says:

But above all, we intend this term to express the theory of a definite
practice. Theological reflection would then necessarily be a criticism of
society and the Church insofar as they are called and addressed by the
Word of God; it would be a critical theory, worked out in light of the
Word accepted in faith and inspired by a practical purpose—and therefore indissolubly linked to historical praxis.[11]

If "orthopraxis" is what I think it is, then in this kind of critical
theory "historical praxis" will interpret the "Word of God," and
not the other way around.[12]

Assuming that this is an accurate analysis of liberation theology's "hermeneutic circle," what are its consequences for both
practical theology and social action? Theologically, since it allows no methodologically relevant distinction between the church
and society, or between theology and ideology, Marxist analyses
of conflict in the latter are just as valid regarding conflict in the
former. A "hermeneutic circle" based on this assumption is entitled to interpret, say, all other forms of practical theology as
reflections of class interests opposed to "solidarity with the oppressed." For example, Jacques Maritain's practical theology of
"integral humanism" thus represents the class interests of the
progressive wing of the national bourgeoisie, the Catholic Action
movements, and the Christian Democratic parties, in which
these interests are organized politically.[13] Once this suspicion is
entertained, theological arguments supporting "integral humanism," for example, the neo-Thomistic metaphysics of "grace and
freedom," need no longer be dealt with discursively. Instead,
they deserve to be exposed in a theoretical reduplication of the
class struggle. But this is only the critical side of a practical
theology based on "orthopraxis." The constructive side consists
in reinterpreting biblical myths and symbols in terms of "liberation." Here, again, the theory-ladenness of "orthopraxis" is cru-

cial. The vision of history carried by the Marxist concept of "praxis" provides the norm for theological reinterpretation. A mixed discourse blending the rhetoric of "salvation" with the dialectics of class struggle results in a strange new *"communicatio idiomatum"* between "liberation" and the Kingdom of God.[14] And this, I argue, amounts to a "politicization" of the "Word of God."

So much for the theoretical consequences of this "hermeneutic circle." The practical consequences for social action, likewise, are both critical and constructive. On the one hand, since the whole realm of theological discourse is now subject to criticism based on "praxis," the church's traditions need no longer exercise any prior restraint upon the strategies and tactics of the "basic communities." While, for example, modern Catholic social teaching has plotted a path equally critical of both "individualism" and "collectivism"—both "free-enterprise" capitalism and Marxist-Leninist socialism—it is now rejected in the name of "orthopraxis" as a mystification of the reality of the class struggle. On the other hand, given the ideological vacuum created by criticizing tradition, the "basic communities" are free to shape their strategies and tactics wholly in response to the requirements of "praxis." But in effect this means that these will be determined primarily by the logic of Marxist analyses of "a revolutionary situation." The result, as Juan Luis Segundo has seen, is not only a theology of liberation but the liberation of theology.[15] And this, I argue, promotes the "politicization" of those who would be doers of the "Word of God."

Once this "hermeneutic circle" is adopted, the religious and moral wisdom of the "mainstream" church can no longer speak with authority to the "basic communities." To allow it to do so would be to betray one's commitment to the oppressed by falling back once more into the ideology of the oppressors. But as I see it, the religious and moral wisdom of the "mainstream" is indispensable precisely for sustaining a sense of Christian identity even within "basic communities." What I mean by this will become clearer, after we examine an alternative to the "orthopraxis" approach.

Model B: Middle Axioms

However misleading the term,[16] the "middle-axioms" approach is a coherent and still promising model for practical theology. First proposed by J. H. Oldham in 1937 in his report to the Oxford Conference on Church, Community, and State,[17] and later elaborated by John C. Bennett in his important but neglected work, *Christian Ethics and Social Policy,*[18] the middle-axioms approach—or something very like it—may be found not only in the writings of major Protestant figures like Reinhold Niebuhr and Paul Tillich but also in the modern papal social encyclicals and the writings of major Catholic figures like Jacques Maritain. What these different perspectives have in common is an approach that promises to establish structures of mutual accountability between the church's "mainstream" and the "basic communities" more effectively than the "orthopraxis" model does. In what follows I will sketch out only as much detail as is necessary to understand this claim.

Middle axioms, as Oldham insists, are meant "to discern the signs of the times,"[19] or in Bennett's words, they "guide us in determining the goals which represent the purpose of God for our time."[20] Thus, even though their intention is similar to that of the "orthopraxis" approach, their differences first appear in what middle axioms presuppose theologically.[21] As Bennett writes, "The Kingdom of God in its fullness lies beyond our best achievements in the world but God does have purposes for us that can be realized."[22] Precisely because the Kingdom is transcendent, "it is very difficult to relate the Christian social imperative to concrete decisions in the political order."[23] While at times it may be necessary for the church "to take sides in a partisan political conflict," Christian witness ultimately remains a ministry of reconciliation.[24] Consequently, Christian social action may take a variety of forms, reflecting both the "direct" and "indirect influence" of the church.[25]

Given these presuppositions, middle axioms help to overcome the "distance"[26] between "our best achievements" and the "fullness" of the Kingdom of God. In seeking both to respect the limits and illuminate the possibilities disclosed by this "distance," they reflect strategies that remain "more concrete than a universal ethical principle and less specific than a program that includes legislation."[27] As Bennett sees them, middle axioms thus form part of a "progression":

> Guiding principles about which there could be no disagreement; a middle axiom which had behind it a substantial consensus but which related Christian decision to a concrete reality . . . about which there could be considerable debate; and finally support of a particular program which was even more ambiguous and about which there was less agreement.[28]

While this progression obviously is nuanced to reflect the different degrees of theoretical consensus and practical authority that can be claimed for Christian social action, of interest here is what it tells us about the relationship of theory and practice in this approach.

Let me illustrate the point using the concerns addressed by liberation theology. Given this progression, "solidarity with the oppressed" would be a "guiding principle" expressing the faith of "prophetic Christianity"[29] common to both the church's "mainstream" and the "basic communities."[30] "Liberation" in its concrete political meaning as revolutionary socialism could be a middle axiom mediating between the two. But so could the kind of "developmentalism" outlined in Pope Paul VI's encyclical *Populorum Progressio*. Finally, the particular programs adopted by the "basic communities" might include providing "infrastructure" for an urban guerrilla movement or doing political canvassing for the Christian Democrats. Thus at each stage of the progression, thorny issues no doubt would emerge. But instead of short-circuiting the discussion of these with indiscriminate appeals to the requirements of "orthopraxis," this approach allows critical reflection to proceed at all three stages. The necessarily controversial decisions made in the third stage of the progression do not preempt discussion of the foundational questions appropriate to the first stage, and vice versa.[31] This more structured approach to theory and practice suggests that in this model the "hermeneutic circle" is drawn differently.

Tradition, rather than "praxis," governs the "hermeneutic circle" in the middle-axioms approach. This is not to say that the traditions of the "mainstream" church are exempt from criticism, but that "prophetic Christianity" generates its own theological "limit-concepts"[32] and these define the framework in which the Marxist mode of analysis or any other critical social theory is appropriated for practical theology. As a result, the middle-axioms approach not only maintains a substantively "Christian social imperative," but also recognizes the different kinds of critical reflection required at each of its stages. For example, the moral ambiguity of certain actions involved in the "basic communities" collaboration with, say, urban guerrilla groups may call for reexamining its own "social practices"[33] and those of the "mainstream" church. If it does,[34] then the very foundations of "prophetic Christianity" may have to be revised. The point, however, is that the church's foundations need not be shaken every time there is controversy over its "social practices" and the actions warranted by them. By distinguishing clearly these three stages of critical reflection, the "hermeneutic circle" in this model becomes at once more nuanced and more stable. As the metaphor of "progression" suggests, it now looks more like a spiral.

There are important theoretical and practical consequences to be noted. Theoretically, this "hermeneutic circle" ensures that the relationship between practical theology and social action always proceeds through the discipline of social ethics. Instead of allowing "praxis" to determine the meaning and tasks of theology, here theology provides a framework in which social practices and actions all lumped together as "praxis" may be subjected to ethical analysis. Christian social ethics, in other words, takes its place in this model as an indispensable form of self-criticism. By contrast, inasmuch as the "orthopraxis" approach repudiates the mediating role of social ethics,[35] its critical function is exhausted in analyzing the ideologies of others. Certain practical consequences follow from the capacity for self-criticism built into the middle-axioms approach. Since it reflects the limits and possibilities symbolized by "prophetic Christianity," in principle it remains alert to the spiritual risks involved in social activism. By refusing to compromise the transcendence of the

Kingdom of God, this approach clearly draws the line between "politicization" and authentic response to the "Christian social imperative." But just as clearly, it draws the line on "excessive spiritualization." Middle axioms continue to be proposed, criticized, and revised not just in spite of, but precisely because of, the ambiguities experienced in social action. In short, this approach does help sustain mutual accountability, because its "hermeneutic circle" remains open to the religious and moral wisdom of "prophetic Christianity."

Eschatological Reserve
It is obvious which model I prefer. But in order to make my choice persuasive, let me conclude by placing the middle-axioms approach in the context of recent controversy over the so-called eschatological reserve.

The "eschatological reserve" refers to the practical and theoretical consequences of uncompromising faith in the transcendence of the Kingdom of God. While it has been formulated differently in a variety of Protestant and Catholic practical theologies, its import is always the same. It signifies the claim that the Kingdom of God relativizes all ecclesiastical theologies and secular ideologies precisely insofar as it is transcendent. It is, in short, the principle of "prophetic criticism" operative in a distinctively Christian "hermeneutic circle." Its consequences for social action are clear and consistent: negatively it rejects the absolutization of any "social practice" as incompatible with the transcendence of the Kingdom; positively, it affirms all "social practices" expressing the "Christian social imperative" as "anticipations" or "analogies" or "outlines" of the Kingdom.[36] The "eschatological reserve," in other words, allows practical theology to draw a distinction between true and false expressions of religious transcendence in social action.

The middle-axioms approach in all its forms embraces the eschatological reserve. Its reasons for doing so were never better dramatized than when Reinhold Niebuhr began to understand how those other twin demons of "cynicism" and "fanaticism" were sapping the very foundations of Christian social action. In the summer of 1934 he wrote an article, "The Problem of Communist Religion," in which he denounced the "political religions" of both the Left and the Right for harboring these demons. Instead of evading the anxieties provoked by these, he proposed to cope with them in an old way that had become refreshingly new. He said:

> It is therefore only religion, the high religion which worships a holy God before whom all men feel themselves sinners, that can maintain the elements of decency, pity and forgiveness in human life and can resist the cruelty and inhumanity which flows inevitably from the process that absolutizes some human values and identifies others with the very source of all evil.[37]

The demonic consequences of absolutizing any political commitment can be overcome, in other words, by remaining faithful to the eschatological reserve. Being a realist, Niebuhr knew that exorcising these demons might also mean a "loss of power" for social activists. But he expressed the hope that this loss would be compensated for by an increase in wisdom, which would better sustain them in their work. Far from symbolizing withdrawal from the struggle, the eschatological reserve represents the possibility of spiritual renewal, even for social activists.

The "orthopraxis" approach sees the matter quite differently. Its reasons for rejecting the "reserve" are expressed most forcefully by Juan Luis Segundo. Since on his assumptions no theological perspective "can be studied with any other final criterion than its impact on praxis,"[38] the "reserve" must be abandoned because it "throws a dash of cold water" on the "enthusiasm" necessary for "real-life revolution."[39] With characteristic bluntness he makes his point: "But who dedicates their life to an 'analogy'? Who dies for an 'outline'? Who motivates a human mass or a people in the name of an 'anticipation'?"[40] Not only is the "eschatological reserve" inadequate to praxis, but precisely its opposite is called for. Given the fact that "absolutization is necessary for effective human mobilization," the "eschatological aspect" can only represent "theology's *way* or manner of accepting absolute commitments."[41] In short, eschatology mediates no religious or moral "content" that would set limits to Christian theory and practice.

Here then the issue is joined between our two models of practical theology. The one based on "orthopraxis" develops a "hermeneutic circle" making it increasingly difficult to recognize the limits imposed by the transcendence of God and his Kingdom. The other presupposes these limits, and tries to formulate middle axioms within an appropriately nuanced view of the ethical role of the church in society. The choice between them boils down to two different ways of seeking the Kingdom of God: is the church to identify its mission with—to use Segundo's idiom—"the practical violence that snatches the kingdom from utopia•and plants it in the very midst of human beings";[42] or is it to maintain a creative tension between its perennial ministry of reconciliation and the occasional need—as Bennett says—"to take sides in a partisan political conflict"?[43]

Given all that we've learned in the past twenty years about the interested nature of ecclesiastical theologies and secular ideologies, this choice truly calls for "discernment of spirits." When I try to respond in light of my own crisis as a social activist, I find that the "orthopraxis" approach lacks the one thing necessary for Christian social action. By rejecting the religious and moral limits symbolized by the "eschatological reserve," it unwittingly promotes precisely the sort of spiritual isolation which, in my experience, conjured up the demons of "politicization" and "excessive spiritualization." Since these not only undermine the "basic communities" capacity for a distinctively Christian witness but also threaten the political effectiveness of social activists committed to it, they are too high a price to pay for any short-term benefits to be gained from a spuriously eschatological "enthusiasm." When, by contrast, I look to the middle-axioms approach, I find not only the one thing necessary, but so much else besides. The principle of "prophetic criticism" provides lessons in humility and faith for those occasions when the demands of social action threaten to overwhelm one's personal identity as a Christian. What can the 1980s still learn from the 1960s? The one thing that social activists like myself failed to learn: a sense of perspective that will allow us to live with the ultimate ambiguity of Christian social action even as we continue to be involved.

NOTES

1. Dennis P. McCann, *Christian Realism and Liberation Theology* (Maryknoll, N.Y.: Orbis Books, 1981).
2. I have taken these terms from Gustavo Gutierrez and Edward Norman. For Gutierrez, "excessive spiritualization" describes the manner in which academic theology has interpreted the Bible. Its error is to base its exegesis on "a kind of Western dualistic thought (matter-spirit), foreign to the Biblical mentality" (*A Theology of Liberation* [Maryknoll, NY: Orbis Books, 1973], p. 166). I am extending the meaning of the term to point out the existential difficulty implicit in retreating into a Neoplatonic religiosity, which apparently minimizes the practical significance of the Incarnation. "Politicization" is defined by Edward Norman as "the internal transformation of the faith itself, so that it becomes defined in terms of political values" (*Christianity and the World Order* [New York: Oxford University Press, 1979], p. 2). My use of the term agrees with Norman's; we disagree, however, regarding the extent to which Latin American theologies of liberation exhibit this difficulty (cf. Dennis P. McCann, *Christian Realism and Liberation Theology*, pp. 234–236).
3. I have chosen these two episodes from the Gospel of St. Mark, because I think they have parabolic significance for understanding the practical significance of the Kingdom of God. Inasmuch as both episodes address the same problem, namely, the subtle relationship between devotion to Jesus and service to the poor, they provide a basis for the theological "limit-concept" discussed further on in this chapter, as the "eschatological reserve."
4. Gutierrez, *A Theology of Liberation*, pp.3–7.
5. Ibid, p. 10.
6. The point is that liberation theology is not a "theology of revolution," but critical reflection in "a revolutionary situation." I have argued elsewhere that liberation theology is deliberately open-ended in the area of ethical analysis, precisely because it seeks to respect the prerogatives of the "basic communities" (cf. McCann, *Christian Realism and Liberation Theology* pp. 209–213). It is appropriate here to record the fact that my criticism of liberation theology does *not* stem from any lack of sympathy towards the aspirations of oppressed peoples for liberation. I question, rather, whether this theology can articulate these aspirations in the way that it seeks to do and still remain integrally theological.
7. I am putting more emphasis on the role of Marxist analysis than some liberation theologians may be prepared to admit. The problem is *not* the use of Marxism to understand the dynamics of social change in Latin America; it is, rather, the way in which Marxism—perhaps unwittingly—becomes the principle of theological hermeneutics through such strategies as Gutierrez's "conscientizing evangelization" and Segundo's "deutero-learning process" (cf. McCann, *Christian Realism and Liberation, Theology*, pp. 156–181, 221–227).
8. My own suspicions in this matter—which are evident in my analysis of Paulo Freire's theory of conscientization, specifically, the connection between his educational theory and what I call the "dialectical vision" (cf. McCann,

Christian Realism and Liberation Theology, pp. 164–172)—have been confirmed by a reading of Nicholas Lobkowicz's *Theory and Practice* (Notre Dame, IN: University of Notre Dame Press, 1967).

9. In Paulo Freire's *Pedagogy of the Oppressed* (New York: The Seabury Press, 1970), the problem of "overdetermination" can be seen in the way he introduces the "generative theme" of "domination"/"liberation" (p. 93). These are asserted as "fundamental . . . for our epoch," but the assertions are apparently based on an existential "wager" of some sort. As far as I can tell, Freire assumes that the themes of "domination"/"liberation" are entailed by the contrast between "nature"/"culture." But this is precisely what I mean by "overdetermination." Not all Marxist analyses exhibit this problem. The work of Jürgen Habermas, I think, represents an attempt to "demythologize" Marxism by subjecting the relationship of theory and praxis itself to critical discussion. His willingness to abandon his earlier theory of an "emancipatory interest" (which would retain both senses of "praxis" in a single concept) in favor of a theoretical "reconstruction" of the claims of "historical materialism" implies recognition of the distinction I'm making here (cf. Dennis P. McCann, "Habermas and the Theologians," *Religious Studies Review* 7, no. 1 (1981), pp. 14–21.

10. Marxists try to get around the "is/ought" problem by asserting the unity of theory and practice. Some of the practical consequences of this move are analyzed in Habermas's critique of Lukacs (Jürgen Habermas, *Theory and Practice* [Boston: Beacon Press, 1973], pp. 28–37). What he says there about the problem of Communist Party organization should be applied to Segundo's "elite of mature Christians," insofar as he models his "elite" on the Leninist notion of a "revolutionary vanguard" (cf. Juan Luis Segundo, *The Liberation of Theology* [Maryknoll N.Y.: Orbis Books, 1976], pp. 208–240).

11. Gutierrez, *A Theology of Liberation,* p. 11.

12. An extended argument for this claim can be found in McCann, *Christian Realism and Liberation Theology,* pp. 156–200.

13. Gutierrez's critique of the "distinction of planes model" exhibits this pattern. (Gutierrez, *A Theology of Liberation,* pp. 53–77). I emphasize the fact that my argument does not imply any *substantive* disagreement with Gutierrez at this point. The problems he discusses are real, and Maritain's metaphysics of grace and freedom is certainly in need of an overhaul. What I object to is the way in which he addresses—or fails to address—the foundational issues implicit in the suspicion that he formulates.

14. *"Communicatio idiomatum,"* of course, designates the rubric for predicating human and divine attributes of the person of Jesus Christ. Thanks to the "hypostatic union," the exchange of human and divine terms is warranted theologically. My metaphorical extension of this notion suggests that a similar predication scheme results from the way in which liberation theology brings together the themes of "liberation" and "salvation." Only in this case, since we are at best speaking of the aspirations of "the people of God" and not of the person of Jesus Christ, I fail to see the warrants for the "hypostatic union" that ensues. What in Christology may be an appropriate expression of the mystery of the Incarnation, in practical theology becomes an inappropriate expression of "politicization."

15. This is the practical outcome of Segundo's conception of "the deutero-learning process" by which "faith" becomes incarnate in a series of "ideologies."

I have argued this point in McCann, *Christian Realism and Liberation Theology*, pp. 221–227.

16. The logical problems suggested by the term "middle axiom" are dealt with in Dennis P. McCann, "A Second Look at Middle Axioms," *The Annual of the Society of Christian Ethics*, *1981*, ed. Thomas W. Ogletree, pp. 73–96.

17. J. H. Oldham, *The Church and Its Function in Society* (Chicago: Willet, Clark & Co., 1937).

18. John C. Bennett, *Christian Ethics and Social Policy* (New York: Charles Scribner's Sons, 1946).

19. Oldham, *The Church and Its Function in Society*, p. 223.

20. Bennett, *Christian Ethics and Social Policy*, p. 76.

21. Both models take their point of departure from "the signs of the times." But liberation theology takes this notion from Vatican II's *Gaudium et Spes* and turns it into an argument for having the right kind of "cognitive instrument" (Juan Luis Segundo, "Capitalism vs. Socialism: Crux Theologica," in *Frontiers of Theology in Latin America*, ed. Rosino Gibellini [Maryknoll, NY: Orbis books, 1979], p. 254) for understanding the class struggle. Bennett and Oldham, on the other hand, place these "signs" in a framework of theological "limit-concepts" which define the scope of the church's role in society. Segundo polemicizes against this strategy, calling it a demand for "signs from heaven" worthy only of "scribes and Pharisees" (Segundo, *"Capitalism vs. Socialism,"* pp. 252–254). Those who would rely on theological limit-concepts for orientation, in his view, are guilty of seeking a religious "certainty" inappropriate to politics. This is not very illuminating in regard to what motivates the middle-axioms approach.

22. Bennett, *Christian Ethics and Social Policy*, p. 77.

23. Ibid., p. 13.

24. Ibid., pp. 89–115.

25. This recognition of a plurality of forms of Christian witness is also to be found in Maritain's discussion of "The Structure of Action" (Jacques Maritain, *Integral Humanism: Temporal and Spiritual Problems of a New Christendom* [Notre Dame: Notre Dame University Press, 1973], pp. 291–308), though the perspectives differ according to the diverging patterns of Protestant and Catholic ecclesiology. Liberation theology apparently has no place for such nuances. Gutierrez's critique of "the distinction of planes model" implies that this pluralism of response is an ideological evasion of the concrete demands of "praxis." He and Segundo differ, however, on whether the goal of liberation theology should be to transform the "mainstream" church or to withdraw an "elite of mature Christians" from it (cf. McCann, *Christian Realism and Liberation Theology*, pp. 213–217). In either case the ecclesiological nuances recognized by the middle-axioms approach would be lost.

26. Bennett, *Christian Ethics and Social Policy*, p. 15.

27. Ibid., p. 77.

28. Ibid., p. 79.

29. Reinhold Niebuhr and Paul Tillich, among others, use this term to describe the normative meaning of biblical faith. The connection between social justice and the righteousness of God emphasized by the Hebrew prophets becomes essential for understanding the theory and practice of Christianity. Liberation theology also appeals to "prophetic Christianity" but sees its role as a principle of ideological criticism differently from what Niebuhr and

Tillich tried to formulate. I have analyzed Niebuhr's approach to the problem of ideology in McCann, *Christian Realism and Liberation Theology*, p. 93–98.

30. It must be understood that neither Oldham nor Bennett explicitly discuss "basic communities." What they have to say about the role of the church in society is, I believe, compatible with my emphasis upon them. The greatest single contribution of liberation theology has been its insistence on the importance of "basic communities" for Christian social action; its greatest single failure, its inability to provide norms governing the relationship between these communities and the "mainstream" church.

31. In recognizing the different levels of critical reflection, the middle-axioms approach conforms in principle to the standards of "communicative competence" ("Vorbereitende Bemerkungen zu einer Theorie der Kommunikativen Kompetenz," in *Theorie der Gesellschaft oder Sozialtechnologie: Was Leistet die System-Forschung?* [Frankfurt am Main: Suhrkamp, 1971], pp. 101–141). I have attempted to apply these standards to theology in an unpublished paper, "Theology as Public Discourse" (McCann, 1980).

32. I use this term in the sense given it in David Tracy's *Blessed Rage for Order: The New Pluralism in Theology* [New York: Seabury, 1975], pp. 91–149). Theological "limit-concepts" are an attempt to formulate the meaning and truth of religious experience and the "limit-questions" to which it gives rise. Methodologically, they presuppose that religious experience has an integrity that can be expressed nonreductively in extraordinary forms of language and discourse. Strictly theological "limit-concepts" are especially useful in conveying what difference—if any—religious experience makes, or should make, to other dimensions of human activity, for example, art, science, morality, in other words, political life in the broad sense of the term. Elsewhere, I try to show the indispensable role of such concepts in practical theology (see *Christian Realism and Liberation Theology*, McCann, pp. 172–180).

33. This term is taken from the work of Stephen Toulmin *(Reason in Ethics* [Cambridge: Cambridge University Press: 1950]) and John Rawls "Two Concepts of Rules," in *Theories of Ethics*, ed. Philippa Foot [New York: Oxford University Press, 1955]). The point is that criticism of "social practices" requires a different strategy of moral discourse from the kind of analysis used to criticize "actions" occurring within the framework of such practices. I believe that this distinction is a most promising alternative to the Marxist concept of "praxis"; and I find something very like it emerging in Habermas's more recent work (cf. Jürgen Habermas, *Communication and the Evolution of Society* [Boston: Beacon Press, 1979]; McCann, "Habermas and the Theologians").

34. Of course, it is possible that the experience of moral ambiguity need not call for a reexamination of "social practices." It may be that the actions must be judged compatible or incompatible with the social practices already adopted. In which case, the social activist may need an examination of conscience to see whether his or her own moral sensibilities are in line with what tradition calls "the dictates of right reason" or what Habermas calls "the formation of a rational identity." Again, the point is that the strategy of critical reflection takes a different form at each stage.

35. The fact that it does so is alleged in McCann, *Christian Realism and Liberation Theology*, pp. 209–211.

36. Cf. Segundo, "Capitalism vs. Socialism," p. 247.
37. Reinhold Niebuhr, "The Problem of Communist Religion," *The World Tomorrow* (1934): 379.
38. Segundo, "Capitalism vs. Socialism," p. 250.
39. Segundo, *The Liberation of Theology*, p. 145.
40. Segundo, "Capitalism vs. Socialism," p. 247.
41. Ibid., p. 256. Segundo's thesis must be understood in the context of his attempt to formulate certain laws concerning "the economy of energy" within human groups (cf. Segundo, *The Liberation of Theology*, pp. 221–228).
42. Segundo, "Capitalism vs. Socialism," p. 257.
43. Bennett, *Christian Ethics and Social Policy*, p. 107.

7. Toward a Theology of Rhetoric/Preaching

LEANDER E. KECK

THE juxtaposition of rhetoric and preaching is intriguing, for it implies the question whether there is any significant difference between a theology of preaching and a theology of rhetoric/ preaching. There is a certain ambiguity here. On the one hand, the combination "rhetoric/preaching" might mean a particular kind of preaching—that which is informed by the art of persuasion. An adequate treatment of this topic would entail a theological understanding of preaching done in a rhetorical way. In this case, "rhetoric" would refer to a particular form, a specific mode of preaching, so that form and content are quite separate. On the other hand, the words "rhetoric" and "preaching" might be used as rough equivalents, especially if we bear in mind that for the ancients rhetoric was a comprehensive term embracing the whole of education and focusing all its aspects on the art of public discourse. Accordingly, because Quintilian (ca. A.D. 35–95) believed that "the art of oratory includes all that is essential for the training of an orator," he urged that the father of the future orator begin the education process from the moment of birth— the baby's nurse should speak properly. Ultimately, the properly trained rhetorician "will have the greatest mastery of all ... departments of knowledge and the greatest power to express it in words."[1]

Preaching too draws on the whole range of theological study and brings the entire enterprise to bear on the art of communicating the gospel. In this sense, "a theology of rhetoric/preaching" would be a theology of theologically informed public discourse. My intent is closer to this latter understanding of the topic than of the former—without going so far as to equate preaching and rhetoric.[2]

Even so, such an undertaking is not without difficulties, especially because the word "rhetoric" itself is burdened with considerable unwanted freight. In ordinary parlance, whatever is associated with rhetoric is immediately suspect. A rhetorical question is often regarded as an unreal question, one posed primarily for effect. A rhetorical discourse is viewed as lacking substance, as a beautiful way of saying little while seeming to say much. When we want to dismiss something we declare it to be "just so much rhetoric!" As one man put it, "If rhetoric is mentioned, one thinks propaganda"[3] Moreover, precisely with regard to preaching, rhetoric is often regarded as at least superfluous, especially for a biblical sermon. Thus Hermann Diem said that "a textual sermon can dispense with rhetorical means of carrying the thought because it is borne by the text."[4] Rhetoric is regarded as an ornament, as when we speak of "a rhetorical flourish." It suggests elocution, oratory, self-conscious performance. Ever since Fosdick, we have emphasized preaching that is pastoral and conversational in style; the well-ordered, eloquently phrased sermon delivered with deliberate attention to inflection is judged to lose precisely what it seeks—effective communication. In a time when we value intimacy and immediacy, a sermon informed by rhetoric puts distance between the preacher and the hearer, calls attention to itself. Besides, we wonder whether there is any point in bringing rhetorical considerations to bear on preaching when the English language is mutilated and precision in expression is widely displaced by a jumble of verbal ejaculations. Surely I am not alone in wondering whether students are being precise when they begin a comment with "I feel like . . ." when one expects them to say "I think. . . ." This recital of difficulties could continue easily enough, but surely these are sufficient to make us realize that the task of considering rhetoric and preaching together is not an easy one.

The irony is that despite considerable emphasis on professionalization of ministry and the acts of ministry, there seems to have been markedly less comparable professionalization of the act of public discourse—that is, a critical and theoretical analysis of what goes on in the act of preaching. Unless I am mistaken, it is the practical, almost technical, suggestions that seem to characterize the feedback in many preaching courses. Increasingly, colleges are emphasizing the development of writing skills, and rightly so, but I detect little comparable movement in the direction of requiring the development of oral communication. As for seminarians, one would surely think that persons being educated for the ministry, a vocation in which articulate oral communication continues to be significant, would be concerned to enhance their ability to speak effectively. But here too I detect no strong tide running toward that shore.

In many quarters, it seems that preaching is no longer valued as highly as in times past, at least if one queries the clergy and their congregations. A recently published study on ministry, based on rather broad statistical data, shows that, overall, North American churches rank preaching (together with leading worship) sixth out of seven dimensions of ministry.[5] One cannot avoid wondering to what extent this is the outcome of a self-selecting clientele—that is, whether current congregations have a relatively low valuation of preaching because they consist largely of persons who are as uninterested in preaching as their preachers. I, at any rate, harbor the suspicion that those who long for effective preaching may have ceased to be part of the congregations that were studied. Yet, there is also a new hunger for effective preaching, and there are signs that seminarians are more interested in learning to preach effectively.

It is well known, of course, that eloquent preaching has never ceased to be practiced and valued among black Christians and among evangelicals of all colors, just as there is a renaissance of interest in preaching among Roman Catholics. At the same time, we who are white Protestants of a more or less "liberal" bent ought not to romanticize the situation among our brothers and sisters, for there too I suspect a reconsideration of the theology of preaching will not be superfluous.

The broader understanding of rhetoric/preaching calls for more than a theological rationale for effective speech arts. It entails nothing less than a reconsideration of the theological bases for preaching at all. It also entails a consideration of the types of public discourse that occur under the name of preaching—apology, meditation, and exhortation, for example. But I shall not develop a taxonomy of preaching acts. I shall concentrate on what appears to me to lie at the center, namely, preaching the gospel—by which I do not mean the so-called evangelistic sermon, but a public discourse in which the gospel comes to articulate verbal expression (thereby leaving aside other art forms by which the gospel can be communicated, like drama, dance, or chant). To pursue this task, I want to explore a piece of rhetoric in the New Testament—Paul's letter to the Romans. Not that Romans contains all that needs to be said. Still, I am persuaded that what it does say, and imply, will suffice to get us moving "toward a theology of rhetoric/preaching." Romans is, in its own way, a theology of rhetoric/preaching.

Rhetoric in the New Testament
Before looking at Romans, it is useful to comment briefly on rhetoric in the New Testament. A concordance will not help us much, for the word *rhetor* occurs but once, in Acts 24:7, which reports that the high priest Ananias, with some elders, arrived in Caesarea with a *rhetor* named Tertullus, who apparently had been hired to argue the case against Paul. The word *rhetor* clearly means something more specific than "spokesman," as the Revised Standard Version renders it; the New English Bible and the Jerusalem Bible have "advocate" and Moffatt has "barrister." The usage in Acts is on target, for one of the major functions of the *rhetor* was to argue cases in court; this was the *Sitz-im-Leben* of the forensic speech, which called for a judgment.

Whether Paul himself should be classified, or would have been, as a rhetorician is not as clear to me as it is to Robin Scroggs.[6] In any case, some Corinthians were saying, "His letters are weighty and strong but his bodily presence is weak and his speech of no account" (2 Cor. 10:10, RSV; *exouthenēmenos* = "despised, despicable"). (He might have been one of those persons who could write a better speech than he could deliver.) In any case, for us Paul's oral communication skill is irrelevant because it is Paul the writer of letters that we know. It should not surprise us that the letters contain so much that is clearly rhetorical. In the first place, Paul (at least according to Acts) spoke publicly in synagogues attended by Hellenistic Jews who, we may safely assume, were conversant with rhetoric, which had long dominated education; in Ephesus, he lectured daily for two years (Acts 19:8–10). The extent to which his preaching and lecturing followed the conventions of rhetoric is not known, since Paul's preaching has not been recorded. Still, because parts of his letters with a rhetorical cast, especially Romans, give the impression that he is putting into writing what he had formulated before, one may assume that he was familiar with the conventions of rhetoric. Moreover, in dictating the letters, he would easily have fallen into patterns and habits of oral delivery, since he knew that the letters were actually surrogate speeches.

Although the rhetorical elements of Paul's letters were noted long ago by Johannes Weiss,[7] relatively little has been done on them in a systematic way until recent years. The new commentary by Hans Dieter Betz on Galatians shows how fruitful this approach can be; the articles by Wilhelm Wuellner, Robin Scroggs, and Robert Jewett, though quite different, are also suggestive.[8] Today, it is not merely the many rhetorical elements within the letters that interest researchers, but the rhetorical character of Paul's arguments, and the overall composition of the letters. A new frontier in Pauline studies will concern Paul's way of combining conventions of rhetoric and epistolography.[9] Still, this is not the occasion to analyze Romans as a piece of Greco-Roman rhetoric. Nor do matters of Greco-Roman rhetoric provide the master key that will unlock all doors in this fascinating house.

In ancient rhetorical theory, there were three major kinds of speeches:[10] the *forensic,* concerned with arriving at a judgment about the past; the *deliberative* (*symbouleutic*), concerned with a course of action to be undertaken; and the *demonstrative* (*epideictic*), commonly associated with public ceremonials when the orator celebrated certain virtues held by the community and manifest in particular events or persons. According to the *Rhetoric to Alexander,* attributed to Aristotle, such speeches were not designed to contest cases but for "display" (*epideixis*).[11] Quintilian associates the epideictic speech with panegyric, which celebrates praise and blame.[12] The "display" or "demonstrative" character of the epideictic discourse should not be taken to mean simply the exhibition of the orator's skills but primarily of the qualities for the subject matter (or person). Indeed, Rosenfield has gone so far as to argue that in hearing epideictic discourse, one had "the opportunity of beholding reality impartially as witnesses of Being," because "when value dwells in the object, it 'cries out' for recognition and remains recognition-demanding regardless of any praise heaped on it"; epideictic "acts to unshroud men's notable deeds in order to let us gaze at the aura glowing from within." It calls for understanding, "the mental activity of free men."[13] In a less laudatory vein, Quintilian says, "the proper function . . . of panegyric [his word for epideictic] is to amplify and embellish its themes."[14]

The extent to which Romans is and is not to be regarded as a piece of epideictic discourse, as Wuellner maintains,[15] needs more investigation. In any case, Romans does not seek to persuade the readers that the gospel is true, for they already believed it. Rather it aims to expand and deepen their grasp of the gospel so that when Paul goes to Jerusalem they will identify with him and subsequently welcome and support him when he arrives in Rome on his way to Spain. Because Romans invites its readers to understand and affirm the gospel which Paul "demonstrates," it is an appropriate basis for our own reflection about preaching, for the heart of any theology of preaching concerns the preaching of the gospel. Romans is not the gospel, the kerygma, but an exposition of the theological basis of the gospel, which is both presupposed and shared with the readers.[16] Perhaps Paul will persuade also his modern readers to intensify their allegiance to the subject matter by the way he amplifies and embellishes its themes.

Romans

In that rhetorically informed speech/letter we call Romans, Paul followed the convention of signaling the content of what was to come by composing a terse, well-formulated paragraph situated between the *exordium* and the *narratio* (development of the argument). It will be the basis of my analysis. Beside, it is appropriate that a chapter on the theology of rhetoric/preaching have a text. And this is it: "For I am not ashamed of the gospel, for it is God's power for salvation for everyone who believes, first to the Jew and also to Greek. For God's righteousness is being re-vealed in it from faith to faith, just as it is written, 'and the one who is righteous by faith shall live'" (Rom. 1:16,17). I want to explore this passage in reverse order. After beginning with some reflection on the relation of scripture and preaching, I turn to the assertion that God's righteousness is being revealed in the gospel, and then to the claim that the gospel is God's power.

Relation of Scripture and Preaching

The appeal to Scripture signals an important aspect of a theol-ogy of preaching, namely, the canon as warrant and criterion. Since I see no reason to retract what I have written on this theme in my book *The Bible in the Pulpit,*[17] I shall draw on what can be read there without attempting to summarize it.

The Bible as canon cannot be separated from the church.[18] Only within the community does it have normative status, be-cause, by a complex process only fragmentarily reconstructable, the church determined that it would have a canon and what its canon would be. What the church canonized, however, was deep-ly rooted in its own life. It is historical criticism that, by circu-itous routes to be sure, has laid bare the multiple ways in which the canon is interwoven with the church from the days of oral tradition right on through to the commissioning of authorized versions in printed form. Throughout this complex history, the Bible's relation to the community has almost always been dialec-tical: on the one hand, the traditions—oral as well as written—that it contains served as warrants for the community's life; on the other hand, those same traditions and texts became the crite-ria of its life. If form criticism revealed how thoroughly the Bible *expresses* the life and faith of the community, redaction criti-cism has disclosed how it *addresses* it as well, how the texts speak against the church. The canon both legitimates and judges the community. Romans—like Hebrews, Mark, or John—both authorizes a particular understanding of faith in Christ and stands over against contrary understandings. My use of Romans in this presentation attempts to be an instance of both functions.

To preach in accord with Scripture is to participate in that process by which the texts' inherent relation to the community is repeated. As I put it in *The Bible in the Pulpit,* to engage in biblical preaching is to do a Bible-like thing. A major function of historical criticism is to expose in detail the amazing range of possibilities, namely precedents, that the canon represents. Exegesis that is alert to the ongoing use and reuse of materials, traditions, themes, and so forth, within the Bible exposes the ways in which the canon embodies a ceaseless process of interpretation, for almost every text is layered in such a way that both the text we have and its antecedents are hermeneutical events in which the community is both warranted and criticized. This means that preaching is faithful to the canon in two ways: in one, the content of the text governs the content of the sermon; in the other, the sermon is engaged in the same dialectical process. Either way, the preacher is first of all an interpreter of canonized tradition. (A text like Romans, which incorporates numerous traditions at the moment of composition, itself had become tradition when it was canonized.)

I need not rehearse the ways in which hermeneutics has come to the fore as a primary task, indeed mode, of theological work. Hans Frei's book, *The Eclipse of Biblical Narrative,* has exposed a deep change: the Bible was the lens through which reality was interpreted but now the lens itself requires interpretation.[19] It has become exceedingly difficult for us to be clear about what it means to interpret any text, and doubly so the canonical texts in our Bible because of their embeddedness in the life and culture of the communities in which they emerged and became canonical. Valuable as the study of hermeneutics is in clarifying what has happened when a text has been interpreted, I cannot rid myself of the suspicion that better hermeneutics does not necessarily lead to better interpretation, but the reverse. If one thinks of the great interpreters of Scripture, in any case, one thing seems to emerge: for them there was something self-evident about the meaning of the text. Whence came that sense of self-evidentness? After the interpretation has occurred one can perhaps trace the factors and plot the dynamics, but often the interpreter, like the writer, does not know whence came the insights. What we can do is to describe the optimum conditions that appear to abet insightful interpretation; but the emergence of black theology and liberation theology have exposed how parochial those descriptions are likely to be. In a word, I suspect that vital interpretation occurs either when the interpreter discovers him-or herself placed between a text and reality, neither of which can be surrendered but must be squared (as when liberal Protestants could not give up either the text or modernity), or when he or she discerns a significant reality through the text. Either way, the interpreter is grasped by that of which (he or she believes) the text speaks. One can explain a text by which one is not grasped, but one cannot interpret it, for interpretation occurs where the interpreter enters into the subject matter of the text deeply enough to be the bearer of its meaning into another context. Such interpretive preaching occurs "as it is written."

Paul, of course, did not preach in accord with Scripture because he regarded it as tradition normatized by the community, but because he believed it to be God's revelation. In the last analysis, we too cannot rest a theology of preaching from the canon only on a phenomenological understanding of texts in communities, but we must grapple with the question of how such a canon is related to God. At this point we shift into another mode of discourse, that of doxology and confession, for to speak of the canon as the vehicle of God's word is to confess that through this text as through none other we have heard a word, experienced reality, in such a compelling way that the Ground of being and value has made itself known. Consequently, this text is now a criterion. Theories of inspiration are but ways of accounting for this by insisting that what the community says about its canon is not a matter of attribution but of grateful acknowledgment set in motion by wonder.[20]

In other words, from one standpoint preaching must be "according to Scripture" because this is the one universally acknowledged norm of the church, and the one to which the church itself is subject. From another standpoint, preaching must be "according to Scripture" because the church has acknowledged this book to be so profoundly and so consistently the vehicle of God's word that whatever cannot be aligned with it lacks the right to be regarded as the vehicle of the word. Preaching that does not regard itself as the instrument of the word ceases to be

Christian preaching, be it ever so interesting, constructive, or even true. This is why Paul, at least, was constrained to show that what he preached was according to Scripture.[21]

God's Righteousness Revealed

We now take up the phrases by which Paul characterizes the gospel, beginning with the claim that in it God's righteousness is being revealed from faith to faith. Since the gospel is the core of all preaching, it is necessary to reflect on what it means for God's righteousness to be revealed in this preached message. Paul's claim is such a suggestive assertion, and so densely packed with revolutionizing implications for preaching, that I can but touch only the most obvious matters.

The first thing that catches our attention is the verb "is being revealed." When Paul speaks of revelation in the gospel, he always has in mind a preached message because the word "gospel" has not yet come to mean written text. Notice especially that he does not say that the gospel is *about* revelation; rather, when the gospel is preached, revelation happens. In what sort of preached message does this occur? For Paul the gospel has its focus in the event of Jesus Christ, seen as a whole and regarded in a particular way. Indeed, at the outset of the letter, he quotes (and modifies) a traditional formulation of the gospel's content: it concerns God's Son, "who was born of the seed of David according to the flesh, (and) who was designated Son of God in power according to the Spirit of holiness by the resurrection from the dead." (Later in the letter, Paul will use other traditional formulations to speak of this event.) The gospel is not simply a report of a revelatory event that had happened in Palestine, but an announcement in which and through which revelation can occur again. Moreover, notice also that Paul uses the present tense— ongoing action in the present. I doubt very much that this is what grammarians call a gnomic present, as in "A stitch in time saves nine." That would make Paul's statement into a maxim. Rather, I think Paul is formulating very carefully a theological claim.

It might be difficult for us to grasp what Paul asserts, unaccustomed as we are to expecting anything to happen in preaching, let alone revelation. Paul does not use the word "revelation" as loosely as we do when we say "that was a revelation to me," meaning "that was a new idea," or a surprise insight. These meanings are there, but they are taken up into a deeper meaning—revelation as a decisive disclosure of transcendant reality. Paul does not claim that *his* preaching is so effective, so rhetorically informed, that it can produce revelatory effects in the hearer. He is not writing about his preaching skill at all, but about what happens when the gospel is preached and believed—revelation occurs that is not to be split off from the revelation that has occurred.

Second, we note what is being revealed—God's righteousness. I shall not rehearse here the recent discussion of the phrase, initiated by Ernst Käsemann.[22] Suffice it to say that in Romans, God's righteousness is God's own rectitude, as 3:21–26 makes clear. This famous paragraph has its climax in the statement that what occurred in the Christ-event happened "in order to prove at the present time that he himself is righteous and that he justifies [or rectifies] the person who has faith in Jesus."

Paul's understanding of righteousness is grounded in the Old Testament, where righteousness means conformity with what is right in a particular relationship. This is clear in the story of Judah and Tamar in Genesis 38. Tamar became a widow and, according to custom, the brother of the deceased was to have fathered children with Tamar in order to provide for her "social security." Because things did not work out this way, Tamar disguised herself as a harlot and seduced her father-in-law, Judah. When Judah found out that she was carrying his child, he said, "She is more righteous than I"—meaning not that she was morally better but that her action was more in accord with what was right in that situation than was his. That is in the right which is in accord with the norm. Righteousness is a term of relationship. But when one speaks of God's righteousness, the norm cannot be some standard independent of God or extraneous to God, but God is the norm of God. Thus God's righteousness is God's faithfulness to God's character. This is why I paraphrase "the righteousness of God" as "the moral integrity of God."

The phrase can also be translated as "the rectitude of God."

This allows us to see the connection between God's character and God's action in a way that our usual translation does not. We have no English verbal form of "righteousness"—we cannot say "righteousify." So we switch to the Latin root and say "justify." Thus the Revised Standard Version translates the line quoted from Romans 3:26 as "that he himself is righteous and that he justifies." But if we use "rectitude" instead of "righteousness," we can bring out the point much better; the Christ-event shows God's rectitude and that God rectifies. Indeed, according to Romans 4:5, it is precisely the ungodly whom God rectifies, whose relationship to himself is made right. God's rectitude manifests itself not in seeing that everyone gets what is deserved, but rather in setting right, in rectifying, the relation between God and the human sinner. The rectitude of God rectifies; it sets relationships right. God comes through as God in making relationships right. Romans 8 shows that the ultimate horizon of this rectification includes creation itself, for it too will be released from wrong relationship to existence, namely having to die. The redemption—or the rectification—of persons *now* is a token of the redemption (or the rectification) of creation *then*. Now we can see what Paul means in our text: when the gospel is preached and believed, God's rectifying rectitude is being revealed—not simply as a new idea about God but as a new reality, definitively disclosed because the new rectified relationship is experienced. This is because whoever believes this gospel *is* rightly related to God.

We may pause to take stock of where we are. If God's rectitude, God's moral integrity, is revealed when the gospel is preached and believed, and if the focal point of the gospel is the event of Jesus Christ climaxed and epitomized by the cross and resurrection, then what is said about Jesus is the word which, when believed, reveals the integrity of God, the Godness of God, the way in which God is most truly God vis-à-vis creation. This implies two things: one, that the message about Jesus is really a message about God (so that we understand why Paul can write that the gospel of God is about God's Son [1:1–3]), and, two, that this message about God is contingent on the Jesus-event. If that is the case, then a theology of preaching must deal with both foci of this ellipse. Ever since Paul, Christian theology has found it impossible to think "God" without thinking "Christ" at the same time, and vice versa, though it has been tried often enough.

It will repay us to look at this a bit more. So closely intertwined are what Paul says about God and what he says about Christ that he not only associates them in phrases like "Grace and peace to you from God our Father and from the Lord Jesus Christ" (1:7), but in Romans 5:8 he can write "God shows [note the tense!] his love for us in that while we were yet sinners Christ died for us." This is near the heart of Paul's theology, and hence is the criterion for his preaching the gospel. Likewise, in Romans 8:3 he writes that God, by "sending his own Son in the likeness of sinful flesh and for sin, he condemned sin in the flesh" (see also Gal. 4:4–6). Similarly, Paul uses the tradition in Romans 1:3,4, which speaks of Christ only in terms of his arrival in history and his transforming departure from it, only of incarnation and exaltation, in order to state the content of the gospel about God.

It is well known that this way of speaking about the decisive event poses formidable problems about Paul's way of preaching, and that he is commonly accused of being disinterested in what we call "the Jesus of history"; this, in turn, raises acutely the question of how we preach the Synoptic Gospels, the traditions they contain, and the events of Jesus' ministry. I cannot deal with that network of questions here; I simply want to share several somewhat apodictic statements. (1) Paul implies that unless Jesus is preached and understood in the context of God's action toward humanity, Jesus will all too readily be preached as law and not as gospel, that theologically there is little difference between preaching the Law of Moses and the Law of Christ because each in its own way leaves the hearer without a revelation of God's rectifying rectitude. For Paul, the revelation of God's rectitude in no way results from the new ideas Jesus may have had. That might have made Jesus the supreme theologian but not a revelatory event. (2) The Jesus-story, capped and epitomized by cross/resurrection, required Paul to rethink the rectitude of God because, for him, the resurrection is not a miracle but a decisive disclosure of whom God vindicates, namely a man who was executed as a sinner and whose execution could be justified by the law itself (Gal. 3:13). In the resurrection God showed himself/herself/itself definitively so that henceforth all thinking of God must come to terms with this event. Consequently, unless Paul was prepared to introduce God into the Jesus-story at the last minute, he had to see the event as God's act from the outset. "Preexistence" was the category that allowed him—and the tradition in which he stood—to do this. (Although the Synoptics lack Paul's category of preexistence, they too, in their own ways, present the Jesus-story as God's act, not as a hero story.) (3) Because those who are grasped by this way of presenting the Jesus-event find themselves rightly related to God, on the one hand, and because also this result cannot be understood as a surprise fallout but only as the intent of God, on the other, Paul (and the tradition) can say that the death of Christ was an act of God's love "for us." An act of love for sinners is an act of grace, and an act of grace is, by definition, an undeserved act, an act of freedom. In short, the Christ-event is the prism through which Paul saw into the radical freedom of God. "The freedom of God" is a phrase never used by Paul, but I am convinced that it is the unstated theme of Romans, and of the gospel, and the sine qua non of all Christian preaching. Without the freedom of God, there is no gospel to preach. Indeed, apart from the freedom of God, the liberation of humanity is illusory.

We have noted that Paul asserts that when the gospel is believed, the righteousness, the rectitude, the moral integrity of God is being disclosed; and we have come to speak of the freedom of God manifested in the Christ-event. How are these related? Actually, they are two ways of speaking of the same thing— the freedom of God is not God's capacity to be arbitrary but the divine ability to be self-consistent over against every human perversion of "God" and of the relation to God. That is what Romans 1:18–3:20 makes clear. Romans 3:27–30 shows that the moral integrity of God, the freedom of God to be God on God's terms, can be distinguished from, but not separated from, the ontic integrity of God: the undifferentiated mode of rectifying the relation of gentiles and of Jews to God (viz. faith) is grounded in the undifferentiated being, the oneness of God. Here Paul writes, "Or is God the God of Jews only? Is he not the God of the gentiles also? Yes, of gentiles also, since God is one; and he will justify [rectify] the circumcised on the ground of their faith and the uncircumcised because of their faith." In short, the freedom of God is a way of speaking of the transcendance of God.

We also noted that Paul understands the gospel to be in accord with Scripture. This means that God's freedom to be self-consonant is not initiated by the Christ-event but clarified and confirmed by it. In the opening sentence of Romans, Paul says that God "'pre-promised' the gospel through his prophets in the holy Scriptures"; consequently the freedom of God includes the capacity to keep the promise, to make good on commitments— which is why Paul must wrestle with the election of Israel in such a way that the parity of Jew and gentile vis-à-vis salvation does not jeopardize the primacy of the Jew. This is also why Paul must rethink the meaning of the law and read the entire Scripture afresh. This is also why the Christian interpretation of Israel's Bible and of Israel's existence is not identical with that of Judaism, while at the same time it also means that the Christian gospel, and the theology in which it is grounded, can never surrender the Bible of the synagogue without falling into Marcionism.

Before going on to the next point, it is useful to pause to reflect briefly on what Paul's understanding of the gospel implies for our own theology of preaching. First of all, it does not summon us to confuse explaining Romans with preaching the gospel; rather, it is the theological criterion for the way the Christ-event is to be preached—as an event in which God has done for us what we cannot do for ourselves, as an event of God's grace. Second, although preaching about God's grace must be distinguished from preaching so that God's grace can happen to the hearer, it is nonetheless true that preaching that reveals God's rectifying rectitude in the hearer's experience cannot eschew theology altogether. At least the theological ground of what is said needs to be clear to the preacher. Because the deepest issues of life are theological, preaching must touch the theological issues, must deal with those dimensions of life in which the hearer's relation to God comes into view. Third, the gospel should be preached in such a way that whoever believes it experiences rectification, knows herself or himself set right with the God committed to making all things right. This implies that the character of God is the substance of a word that comes home to the hearer as a life-aligning event. Just as the revelation of God's rectitude in the gospel is not split off from the original revelation while not simply continuous with it, so the freedom of God in the Christ-event is not split off from the freedom of God in the preaching event. Just as the Christ-event was the power by which the tyranny of sin and death was broken, so the gospel is the power of God by means of which the hearer is rescued and rectified.

The Gospel as God's Power

Having noted briefly the relation between the gospel and Scriptures and having explored the assertion that God's moral integrity is revealed when the gospel is believed, we now turn to Paul's claim that the gospel is God's power for everyone who believes. Paul does not say that the gospel is *about* God's power. That would make the gospel a piece of information that our technologically minded culture would immediately turn into a news report of how God's power could be used. Rather, Paul asserts that the gospel *is* God's power to effect salvation for everyone who entrusts himself or herself to God as proclaimed in the news about the Christ-event. Our task, therefore, is to understand how this message is power. By this daring assertion, Paul answers our question, "Why preach?" It also implies an answer to the question of how rhetoric is related to preaching.

We pick up this web of issues by reflecting on the matter of faith, which binds together each of the three topics we have been exploring: the righteous live by faith, God's integrity is revealed in the gospel from faith to faith, and the gospel is God's power for those who have faith. Paul's theology of preaching emphasizes both the freedom of God to be faithful and the faith-response of the hearer. Only where the gospel elicits faith is what is said about the gospel true, namely that it is God's power, and that in it God's rectifying rectitude is being revealed. (This is not the same as saying that only when the gospel is believed is it true.) If we follow the grain of Paul's thought, we must say that whoever preaches the gospel must be prepared to elicit, nurture, and clarify faith. Otherwise the gospel will not be known as God's power, and neither salvation nor the revelation of God's transcendent freedom to rectify will be experienced.

What is faith and why is it decisive? I continue to hold that what I said in *A Future for the Historical Jesus*[23] is valid, namely that faith is the entrustment of the self, and that most of what is meant by "faith" can be expressed better by the word "trust" because this is both a verb and a noun, whereas we have no verbal form for the noun "faith." More important, trust is constitutive of the self, especially when the self is understood relationally. My identity is constituted by a network of trusts across time; who I am is determined by whom and what I trust and distrust, by the realities I deem trustworthy and untrustworthy. Consequently, what and whom I trust is inseparable from the way I perceive and construe the trusted and the distrusted, the trustworthy and the untrustworthy. Trust is more than assent of the mind; it is also allegiance of the self; it involves the affections and passions no less than the reasonings of the mind. The ultimate ground of what and whom we deem trustworthy is what we call "God," the Ground of being and value. Consequently, when preaching calls for faith/trust, it does not ask for something to begin absolutely, but for a realigning of the trusting we already do.

It would be a mistake to assume that this realigning is mostly a matter of fine tuning. Paul, at any rate, understands it much more radically, even though "repentance" (turning around toward God, conversion) is not part of his working vocabulary in his letters. Romans 1:18–3:30 makes clear just how radically this realignment is to be if the relation to God is rectified. Moreover, if God is the final Ground of values, and if values are socially formed and acquired, then the restructuring of the relation to God by trust implicates the restructuring of social relationships as well, so that there is no hiatus between "faith" and "ethics."

Now we can understand why Paul says that those who entrust themselves to the God of the message about Christ, experience the gospel as God's power. In short, only that message has the capacity to redirect our trusting in such a way and at such a level that we are emancipated, rescued, saved, from trusting the unworthy at the core of the self. No one, of course, undertakes to trust the untrustworthy; everyone trusts what is deemed to be trustworthy just as one distrusts what is perceived to be untrustworthy. In other words, the configuration of trust and distrust implies a judgment about the object of trust or distrust (and all the mutations in between). The fact that Paul says that the gospel is God's power to rescue everyone who believes it means that he assumes that everyone, Jew no less than gentile in Paul's context, needs rescue from misplaced trust or from trusting a misconstrued "object of trust"—which amounts to the same thing, for one cannot rightly trust someone or something that is misconstrued. (Here is the central reason why preaching must not eschew theology, for I can no more be rightly related to—that is, trust—a misconstrued God than I can be rightly related to my misconstrued wife or son or friend.) Moreover, one is not aware that trust is misplaced or the object of trust misconstrued apart from an event or a word that discloses an alternative. Put in more formal theological idiom, it is salvation that discloses the true nature of sin, just as it is health that reveals illness, perfect pitch that discloses what is off-key. This is why the gospel, focused on God's act in the Christ-event, *is* the emancipatory power when it is believed.

If this emancipating power is experienced only when the gospel is believed, then it is also true that the gospel is believed only when it is communicated and heard. In Romans 10:14–15 Paul is explicit: "But how are persons to call upon him in whom they have not believed? And how are they to believe in him of whom they have never heard? And how can they hear without a preacher?" Preaching is necessary because, as Paul says two verses later, "Faith comes from hearing [not simply "from what is heard" as the RSV has it], and hearing comes by the word of Christ"—that is the speech whose content is Christ. This entrustment of the self to God is not the result of an inference, but is a response to a word, an interpreting word about who God is shown to be by the Christ-event.

Paul does not say so, but we are surely consonant with what

he does say if we see here a tacit justification for the use of rhetoric, or persuasion that moves the self as a self. What I have in view is Paul's clear perception that not only are we already enmeshed in patterns of trust and distrust, but that these patterns are so strong that they are a form of bondage. Romans 1 makes clear that for gentiles this is bondage to idolatrous confusions of creature and creator, just as Romans 2 makes clear that for Jews it is bondage to misconstrued election. In these chapters Paul also shows that there are moral consequences of confusion about God just as moral confusion has epistemic consequences for the knowledge of God. Long before moderns began discussing ideology, and "interest," and the sociology of knowledge, Paul saw the moral dimension of the knowledge of God or of what is taken to be knowledge of God. What Paul glimpses here is really the theological basis for public discourse that exposes the character of the culture's and the church's distortions of the reality called "God"—distortions grounded in the perversion of the transcendance of God into the superior power of our particular patron. In Romans, Paul deals twice more with the human condition: in chapter 5 he writes of the Adamic situation, and in chapter 7 of the plight of the persons who try to establish a right relation to God by achieving minimum requirements—the Mosaic situation. Given the power of the entrustments already in place, the word of Christ must be presented as persuasively as possible. Rhetoric serves the preaching of the gospel, in other words, when it aids the preacher in appealing to the total self— to the affections no less than to the mind, to the will, and to the imagination. People should not be exhorted to believe, for that turns faith into an achievement. But they can be moved to entrust themselves to the God of the gospel by strategies that not only respect the integrity of the self but appeal to the self in a way that enhances it. The fact that rhetoric is vulnerable to becoming manipulation no more forbids the use of rhetoric than faith's vulnerability to becoming superstition disallows faith.

This brings us to the line with which Paul began his paragraph: "Therefore I am not ashamed of the gospel"; this is a rhetorical way of saying, "I am proud of the gospel," or "I have full confidence in it." Why? Because by believing it, one experiences it as God's power. Why? Because God's rectifying rectitude, God's freedom to keep faith with God's character on God's terms, is being disclosed whenever a believing person is rectified, set right with the Creator. All this accords with Scripture once you know what to look for.

Those who are persuaded by Paul's *epideixis* will share his pride and confidence in the gospel, and so renew their estimate of preaching, and perhaps their preaching as well. Preaching, of course, is not the whole of the ministry and never was—not even for Paul. He was, after all, a pastor as well, and in his own way an educator too, as well as an astute strategist in mission. Charismatic and yet earthy, irrascible and yet sensitive, caustic and yet tactful, Jewish to the marrow yet ardent champion of gentile Christians because he penetrated to the fundamentally human that relates everyone to God, this controversial emissary of Christ appears to have been the first Christian to have written a theology of preaching. The power of what he said is not derived from his priority in time, but from his penetration into the theme. He was proud of the gospel because he discovered that he could trust it not only for his salvation but also for his theology, including his theology of preaching. In the last analysis, I know of nothing that the church today needs more than learning to share Paul's confidence that the gospel is nothing to be ashamed of.

Nor is preaching that is informed by the art of rhetoric.

NOTES

1. Quintilian, *Institutio oratio* I Pref; cited from Loeb Classical Library ed. vol. 1.
2. Such an equation, proposed by Gert Otto in *Predigt als Rede: Über die Wechselwirkungen von Homiletik und Rhetorik* (Stuttgart/Berlin/Cologne/Mainz: 1976), has evoked considerable discussion in Germany; see Ulrich von den Steinen, "Rhetorik—Instrument oder Fundament christlicher Rede?" *Evangelische Theologie* 39 (1979): 101, n. 3.
3. H. J. Schulz, "Wird Rhetorik gesagt, so wird Propaganda gedacht." Quoted in Ulrich von den Steinen, "Rhetorik—Instrument oder Fundament christlicher Rede?" *Evangelische Theologie* 39 (1979): 105.
4. Hermann Diem, "Warum Textpredigt?" Quoted in Hans-Georg Wiedemann, "Zur rhetorischen Gestaltung der Predigt," *Evangelische Theologie* 32 (1972): 39.

5. David S. Schuller, Merton T. Strommen, and Milo L. Brekke, eds., *Ministry in America* (San Francisco: Harper & Row, 1980), p. 25.
6. "Paul as Rhetorician: Two Homilies in Romans 1–11," in Robert Hammerton-Kelly and Robin Scroggs, eds., *Jews, Greeks and Christians* (W. D. Davies Festschrift), (Leiden: E. J. Brill, 1976), p. 273.
7. Johannes Weiss, "Beiträge zur paulinischen Rhetorik," in *Theologische Studien* (Bernhard Weiss Festschrift), (Göttingen: 1897), pp. 165–247.
8. Hans Dieter Betz, *Galatians*, Hermeneia Series (Philadelphia: Fortress, 1979). Wilhelm Wuellner's article, "Paul's Rhetoric of Argumentation in Romans: An Alternative to the Donfried-Karris Debate Over Romans," is now included in the collection edited by Karl P. Donfried, *The Romans Debate* (Minneapolis, MN: Augsburg, 1977), pp. 152–174. Scroggs's article (see note 6) uses rhetorical considerations to carry out a source critical analysis: Romans 1–11 combines two speeches. Robert Jewett, "Romans as an Ambassadorial Letter," *Interpretation* 36 (1982): 5–20, undertakes to refine Wuellner's arguments. The antithetical formulations have been studied recently by Norbert Schneider, *Die rhetorische Eigenart der paulinischen Antithese* (Tübingen: J.C.B. Mohr [Paul Siebeck], 1970).
9. For an excellent introduction to the epistolographic traditions, see William G. Doty, *Letters in Primitive Christianity* (Philadelphia: Fortress, 1973), where the most important literature on the topic can be found.
10. Quintilian reports that the number of types of speeches was a disputed matter, but he prefers the three that were traditional ever since Aristotle. *Institutio oratio* III 4.
11. *Rhetoric to Alexander* XXXV; Loeb ed., p. 405.
12. Ibid.
13. Lawrence W. Rosenfield, "The Practical Celebration of Epideictic," in E. E. White, ed., *Rhetoric in Transition* (University Park/London: Pennsylvania State University Press, 1980), pp. 131–156.
14. Quintilian, *Institutio oratatio* III 7:6; Loeb ed., vol 2, p. 467. Harry Caplan, the translator of the Rhetorica ad Herennium, attributed to Cicero, notes that in epideictic oratory the "primary purpose is to impress . . . ideas upon them [the hearers], without action as a goal." Cicéro I, p. 173, note 6.
15. Wuellner, "Paul's Rhetoric of Argumentation in Romans."
16. For a survey of the various ways in which the New Testament speaks of the gosepl, see Christoph Burchard, "Formen der Vermittlung christlichen Glaubens in Neuen Testament," *Evangelische Theologie* 38 (1978): 313–40; for Paul, 315–20.
17. Leander Keck, *The Bible in the Pulpit* (Nashville, TN: Abingdon, 1978).
18. For a useful discussion of the canon, see the October 1975 issue of *Interpretation*, which is devoted to the theme. The important literature can be found there.
19. Hans Frei, *The Eclipse of Biblical Narrative* (New Haven, CT: Yale University Press, 1974).
20. For an insightful discussion of this theme, one emphasizing the continuity of inspiration not only throughout the formation of Scripture but also in its ongoing interpretation in preaching, see Paul J. Achtemeier, *The Inspiration of Scripture* (Philadelphia: Westminster, 1980), especially chaps. 5 and 6.
21. The recent article by Richard R. Caemmerer, Sr., "Why Preach from Biblical Texts," *Interpretation* 35 (1981): 5–17, does not deal with canonicity of

precisely the sort of literature the Bible contains. The entire issue (January) is devoted to biblical preaching.

22. Ernst Käsemann, "'The Righteousness of God' in Paul," in *New Testament Questions of Today* (Philadelphia: Fortress, 1969), pp. 168–182.

23. Leander Keck, *A Future for the Historical Jesus* (Nashville, TN: Abingdon, 1971; paperback ed., Fortress, 1981).

8. Practical Theology and the Shaping of Christian Lives

JAMES W. FOWLER

In 2 Corinthians 5:20 Paul writes: "So we are ambassadors for Christ, God making his appeal through us." Just prior to this Paul has summed up the entirety of the promise of the Christian gospel—the Christian *new*—with this claim:

> If anyone is in Christ, that person is a new creation; the old has passed away, behold the new has come. All this is from God, who through Christ reconciled us to himself and gave us the ministry of reconciliation. That is, God was in Christ reconciling the world to himself, not counting their trespasses against them, and entrusting to us the message of reconciliation.

He continues:

> so we are ambassadors for Christ, God making his appeal through us. We beseech you on behalf of Christ, be reconciled to God. For our sake God made him to be sin who knew no sin, so that in him we might become the righteousness of God. (2 Cor. 5:17–21, RSV)

The goal of all Christian education, the purpose of formation in the community of Christian faith, is—by the grace and power of God's lively presence in the Holy Spirit—to form men and women through whom God can afford to make his appeal in the world. The formation and transformation of persons at which the practice of Christian nurture aims have to do with grafting men and women into Christ. In the identification represented in this grafting, we grow in acceptance of the reconciliation with God brought about in Christ, and the *vocation* to become ambassadors—agents—of that reconciliation in the world.

There is a danger that we may hear these formulations about

ambassadorship and being grafted into Christ too narrowly, as though conversion to and formation in Christ were somehow antithetical to being human. There is a danger that we may regard this avowedly Christocentric point of beginning our reflections on practical theology and education as setting up barriers of exclusivism and privileged superiority over against a pluralistic world. To move in these ways would represent a betrayal of the Incarnation, and to make of the church a bounded end in itself rather than to see it as a servant and means to an end. God's self-giving in Christ—Godhood taking on flesh in a genuine and true humanity—invites us and all the world into full humanity. The reconciling love and work of God, eminently and fully focused in the life, death, and resurrection of Jesus, the Christ, does not aim at the creation of little—or great—conventicles of a withdrawn elite. Rather it aims at the liberation and restoration of humankind for full humanity, and for fitness to be citizens in the reign of God—citizens in the justice and shalom of God. It is for this Kingdom of God that we are called to be ambassadors.

Toward a Characterization of Practical Theology

"Practical Theology," Schleiermacher wrote in his *Brief Outline of the Study of Theology,* "is only for those in whom an ecclesial interest and a scientific spirit are united." Schleiermacher's felicitous joining of "ecclesial interest" and "scientific spirit" points rightly to the integrity and the dialectic at the heart of practical theology. *Practical theology* is theological reflection and construction arising out of and giving guidance to a community of faith in the praxis of its mission. Practical theology is critical and constructive reflection on the praxis of the Christian community's life and work in its various dimensions. As such, practical theology is not self-sufficient as a discipline. Though it has and must exercise direct access to the sources of faith and theology in Scripture and tradition, it does not do so in isolation. Practical theology is part of a larger, theological enterprise that includes the specialities of exegetical, historical, systematic, and fundamental theological inquiry and construction.

It is a mistake to assume that practical theology is merely a derivative from exegetical, historical, or systematic studies. The unfortunate term "applied theology" seems to suggest that practical theology amounts to taking the creative results of other subdisciplines of theological work and merely drawing their implications for the tasks of ministry and mission. Even the term "practical theology," when used in the manner that bifurcates theory and practice so as to see the former as creative and authoritative, and the latter as merely derivative and pragmatic, can be grievously misleading. Through the work of liberation theologians who have taken seriously Marx's recovery of the Aristotelian and Hegelian notion of praxis and through its introduction into philosophical theological inquiry by David Tracy and others,[1] we are learning to get beyond the dichotomizing of the theoretical and the practical. (As one who has labored for a decade on a theory of faith development I have always appreciated Kurt Lewin's terse dictim that "there is nothing so practical as a good theory.")

Practical theology, rightly pursued, does its work in the convergence point of several crucial interactions. First, it is moved toward engagement and service in the world by the initiatives of God in forming and liberating a covenant community, and in intensifying and universalizing that covenant through the Christevent. Though practical theology has no unmediated access to the constitutive events by which God's initiatives came to expression, its access to the resulting records and lore is as direct as that of any other of the theological subdisciplines. In the evolving division of theological labor, however, practical theology has come to rely on exegetical, historical, and systematic studies for testing the validity of its own direct interpretations of the sources, and for discoveries and directions that will enrich and correct its own appropriations. In its relation to the records of God's initiatives toward humankind I am suggesting that practical theology stands in a trialectical relation. It relates directly to the sources of faith and theology, on the one hand, and it relates to the results of the specialized subdisciplines of theological inquiry into these sources on the other. A chart, on which we may build, might help make this clear:

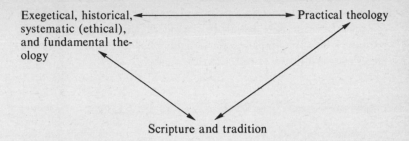

Notice that all the arrows are double-directional, suggesting that the exchanges are in fact dialectical. The traffic between the three partners here is two-way in every instance. Looking at these matters in this way helps us to see why it is a historical and categorical mistake to characterize exegetical, historical, systematic, and fundamental theology as the "classical" theological disciplines and to think of practical theology as the more recent innovation. Actually all theological inquiry was *practical* in any "classical" period we know about. Only with the rise of the university as the prime locus of theological research did the various subfields of theological inquiry gradually differentiate and become separated from the context, issues, and controlling focus of pastoral and ecclesial concerns.[2]

Now let me focus our attention on another set of trialectical relations in which practical theology engages as it does its work. Here I have in mind the practical theological concern for understanding and shaping initiatives in the church's present experiences of social, cultural, political, economic, and personal realities. Practical theology worries with the points of engagement between the disclosures and imperatives released in the sources of faith, and the particular present shape of the calling of the faithful. In this effort to grasp the shape of the church's present calling, practical theology enters into dialogue with those disciplines that have evolved to provide hermeneutical perspectives on social and personal experience. Again, practical theology has as direct access to the data of present experience as do any of these partner disciplines. From theology it brings its own distinctive hermeneutical images and lenses. But to do its work adequately practical theology carries on critical conversation with the social sciences, the arts, and literature. If we add this second trialectic to our chart we begin to see the unique focus and integrity in the broad responsibilties of practical theology:

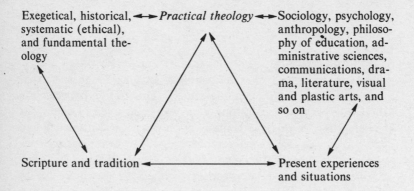

Exegetical, historical, ←→ *Practical theology* ←→ Sociology, psychology,
systematic (ethical),   anthropology, philoso-
and fundamental the-   phy of education, ad-
ology   ministrative sciences,
                                                     communications, dra-
                                                     ma, literature, visual
                                                     and plastic arts, and
                                                     so on

Scripture and tradition ←——————————→ Present experiences
                                              and situations

In reflecting on this chart, however, we also see why contemporary practical theology always flirts with the risk of being like the North Platte River—a mile wide and an inch deep. Or why present-day departments of practical theology, organized around the various subdimensions of ecclesial praxis, so frequently lack a felt sense of disciplinary integrity. Nevertheless, this diagram helps us to see what a critically valuable member of the theological community a competent practical theologian can be. While off to the left of our chart the exegetes and other theologians are consorting with linguists, hermeneutical theorists, historiographers, philosophers, and phenomenologists, the practical theologians' interdisciplinary contribution is to participate in lively ways in the conversation between theology and one or another of the social sciences or the arts.

The practical theologian does not, however, work at interdisciplinary inquiry for its own sake or for the sake of *theoria* (understanding) alone. Her or his broader commitment lies in the direction of bringing interdisciplinary resources to bear in critical and constructive perspectives on some dimension or dimensions of ecclesial praxis. Here we return to Schleiermacher's *scientific spirit* in its linkage with *ecclesial interest*.

If we return to our chart now we can complete it by bringing ecclesial praxis, in its various dimensions, into the picture. I prefer the term *dimensions* rather than *functions* to describe the aspects of ecclesial existence that focus the concerns of practical theology. *Dimensions* comes closer, I think, to suggesting the organic inter-relatedness of the various aspects of ecclesial ministry, lay and ordained, in and beyond the community, than does the notion of functions. Functions might suggest distinct, separate or bounded areas of ministry. (There is a sense, I believe, in which the dimensions identified here do represent "functional imperatives" for any community that is to survive with quality, renew itself with new members, conserve and extend its traditions, and have any impact on the larger social-cultural-political ecology of which it is a part.)

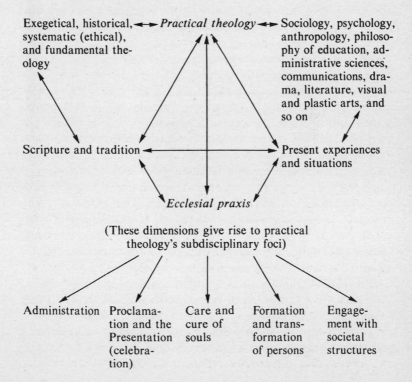

Exegetical, historical, ←→ *Practical theology* ←→ Sociology, psychology, systematic (ethical), and fundamental theology — anthropology, philosophy of education, administrative sciences, communications, drama, literature, visual and plastic arts, and so on

Scripture and tradition ←————————→ Present experiences and situations

Ecclesial praxis

(These dimensions give rise to practical theology's subdisciplinary foci)

Administration   Proclamation and the Presentation (celebration)   Care and cure of souls   Formation and transformation of persons   Engagement with societal structures

We began this outline characterization of practical theology with a definition. Practical theology, we said, is theological reflection and construction arising out of and giving guidance to a community of faith in the praxis of its mission. It is "critical and constructive reflection on the praxis of the Christian community's life and work in its various dimensions."

Plainly, I have assumed here that while persons who do practical theology may also address other audiences and engage in other intellectual enterprises, insofar as they work as practical theologians they do so in relation to and on behalf of a faith community and its praxis. And because theology is an enterprise carried on more by Christians than by persons in other religious traditions (who have other dominant ways of awakening vision and commitment, and of giving shape to personal and communal life) I make reference solely to Christian practical theology.

Further, as the central axis linking practical theology and ecclesial praxis in the last chart suggests, I believe that the enterprise of practical theology draws its energy and experiences its primary vocation in relation to the concrete *ecclesia*. While I am convinced that other subdisciplines of theology, most notably among these fundamental theology, address other audiences than ecclesial ones and may be said to focus their concern in other than ecclesial directions, theological inquiry in all its subdisciplines draws its most fundamental impetus, I believe, from ecclesial passion. (This is not to be equated with *clerical* passion.)

Practical theology lives close to the crucibles in which the power of religious symbols and language vindicate themselves as indispensable in the grasping and illumination of the depths of our experiences of limit, threat, goodness, and grace. Practical theology keeps the theological disciplines in close range of those arenas where the re-presentation or actuality of divine disclosure events occurs, so as to give freshness to the need for and the point of systematic reflection on faith's meanings.

Practical theology aims at a kind of knowing that guides *being* and *doing*. While concerned with theory, it is not *theoria;* while concerned with techniques, it is not *poiesis*. Its knowledge is a *practical knowing*—a knowing in which skill and understanding cooperate; a knowing in which experience and critical reflection work in concert; a knowing in which disciplined improvisation, against a backdrop of reflective wisdom, marks the virtuosity of the competent practitioner.[3]

Formation and Transformation in Faith

Our overview of the tasks and resources of practical theology has helped us locate the place of education as a dimension of ecclesial life and as a focal area of practical theology. I have designated this dimension as the church's concern with the *formation and transformation of persons*. *Education* is a suitable word to describe this concern, but only if we do not reduce it to *schooling* or equate it too narrowly with *catechesis* or *instruction*. If we understand education in the more comprehensive sense suggested by the German term *Bildung,* then the process it denotes will include the variety of informal and formal ways, beyond instruction and catechesis, in which ecclesial communities intentionally sponsor the awakening and formation of persons in faith. I want us to think of education in this broader, more dynamic and interactive sense.

I turn now to the effort to sketch some of the foundations for a practical theology of formation in Christian faith. As my introductory overview intended to show, practical theology investigates Scripture and the tradition, on the one hand, and the shape of the present situation of ecclesial ministry, on the other, for the sake of constructive and critical guidance of the church's praxis. Any proper prolegomenon to a practical theology taken as a whole would require a full-blown doctrine of the church, worked out in correlation with a coherent and comprehensive systematic theology. Such a prolegomenon is far too big an undertaking for our present purposes. There may be legitimacy, however, in starting at the other end. If practical theology is committed to a praxis methodology, then it makes sense to narrow our focus to the churchs' concern for the formation and transformation of person toward Christian faith, and to think through the goals, methods, and theological foundations of that praxis.

Our opening reference to Paul's passage about being ambassadors for Christ points with clarity and power to the guiding goal of Christian formation. Our intent, in the investment of human effort and in trusting in the empowering guidance of God's living spirit, is to form men and women by whom God can afford to make his appeal in the world. Put in broadest terms, our goal is to call forth and nurture persons who taste and see the sovereign love of God as constitutive of all that is, and who come to make being partners with God, in his present and in-breaking reign, the fundamental option of their lives.

I see four principal constituent elements required for a practical theology of Christian formation adequate for this goal. I shall describe these four foundational elements, indicating in each case the directions I would propose to go in marshaling them. After sketching the outlines of the four foundational elements I want to consider a few of the questions of theological method posed by the present state of the discussion in the field of practical theology.

The first foundational element needed for a practical theology of Christian formation is *a theory of God's sovereign love as the pattern of action underlying and giving character to the cosmic process.* What is God doing? What is God being-toward? How can we discern the divine character and action in the welter and crossfire of all that impinges upon us? When we take seriously Jesus' preaching about the in-breaking reign of God, where do we look in order to discern and to respond to it? Theology is always constructive and critical reflection on God-in-relation-to-humanity and on our experience of the world. We have no other point of vantage for reflection. Therefore, any helpful theory of God's sovereign love must illumine the ground and the larger contours of our lived experience. Further, any theory of God's sovereign love that is Christian and biblical must illumine and fulfill our memories of the disclosure events that formed and oriented our forebears to the future as God's future. And it must help us see the solidarity in which we stand with all persons from the past and present, by virtue of our being-toward the universal future that God unifies and intends.[4]

In the early years of his teaching at Yale, H. Richard Niebuhr hammered out the outlines of a theology of the sovereignty of God that seems to me both faithful and foundational for Christian seeing and being. I think that Niebuhr's three principal metaphors for God's ways of being in relation to humankind are biblically informed and illuminative of fundamental human experience. Each of the major metaphors has an analogue of response and partnership for human beings. At the heart of his courses on Christian ethics, Niebuhr focused on Response to God the Creator, Response to God the Ruler or Governor, and Response to God the Redeemer and Liberator.[5] At times Niebuhr wrote and spoke of God the Creator as the Source and Center of Being and Value (all that *is* has *being and value* in relation to this moving Source and Center). This idea is close in ways to Tracy's suggestion that we should speak of God as the "eminently relative one"—the divine relativity in relation to which all being is relative.[6]

The human vocation in response to *God as Creator* is that of co-creation and conservation. We are called to imitate God's creativity. Not in specific acts of duplication, but by becoming ourselves authors of novelties that enrich, augment, or conserve being. Ethically we are called to center our valuing in God and to decenter from the perspectives of and idolatrous attachments to our group or individual egos.

Underlying the metaphor of *God as Governor or Ruler* is the image of God as the "structuring-intending-righteousness" in the universal process, and in human and world history as part of that larger process. Niebuhr was never directly anthropomorphic in his development of this metaphor. Yet he witnessed to an analogy between the brilliant politician (Lincoln was a favorite example), who could orchestrate the narrow self-interests and cussedness of little men so as to achieve great goals, and the God who incorporates even our grievous misuses of our freedom into the ultimate realization of his Kingdom. The human vocation in response to God's governing action is to become partners in constructing and maintaining social relations of justice and peace.

The third principal metaphor that Niebuhr employed for God's sovereign and loving action is *God the Redeemer and Liberator.* Sin as wrong love and egocentric creativity sets us at enmity with God. Sin as the refusal of partnership in justice and righteousness hardens into structures of self-aggrandizement and retaliation by nations, groups, and persons. God as Redeemer and Liberator in Jesus the Christ submits to the destructiveness present in the structures of self-valuing and to the brutality in the defensive forces of self-aggrandizement and retaliation. The cross brings to culmination a double revelatory disclosure: in the death of Christ God's unlimited love for his creatures is shown forth and poured out. And in the cross, where innocence and goodness are torn apart, we see the disclosure of the perversions and the ultimate poverty of all that which, from the standpoint of sin, seems to be good and powerful. In the cross goodness and love are disclosed; evil and perversion are unmasked. The human vocation in response to God's action as Redeemer and Liberator is that of acceptance and identification. Through God's redeeming and liberating love in Jesus Christ we are called into partnership with God to be about the liberation of his people and the anticipatory realization of his rule. We are called to be among those persons by whom God can afford to make his appeal in the world.

The second constituent element needed for a practical theology of Christian formation is to be found in the direction of what has come to be called *faith development theory.* In the intentional effort to sponsor persons toward an informed fundamental option for partnership with God many questions of practical moment arise. To what degree are the pre-images of faith, formed in infancy (and perhaps beginning prenatally), foundational for the vulnerabilities and strengths of a person's later faith? What forming power do ritual, visual symbols, and narrative exert on the faith of children, of adolescents, of adults? How are faith and moral development related? What quality of commitment can fairly be expected of persons at different stages in the life of faith? How do persons compose their experiences of knowing and loving God, or approach the discernment of God's presence, in different eras of their lives? Are there stages of faith?

Practical theologians are beginning to take account of a different kind of pluralism that our usual understandings of the term suggest—a pluralism that epistemologically oriented lifespan developmental theories are helping us to see. In any typical audience of adults one addresses, in addition to the pluralism arising from different religious traditions or social class, from contrasting temperaments, or from varying sensitivities and value commitments, there will be three or perhaps four different "styles" of construction employed in their making sense of what you say. It is not just the *contents* of our consciousnesses that differ. The underlying operations of thought, of valuing, of composition and questioning that constitute our consciousness work in accordance with different operational rules. My own research and reflection lead me to believe that while we each have a most advanced or developed style of consciousness, other earlier and less developed styles continue to be operative in our constructions of meaning and can become dominant at particular moments.

Of special interest for a practical theology of formation are the new qualities of strength and challenge made possible through the successive construction of emerging new structural styles in faith. In early childhood, for example, the imagination, now resonant with and stimulated by language and other symbols, can form powerful and long-lasting images which orient the child and fund later development and reflection. In childhood proper, narrative arises—the ability to generate stories that grasp, conserve, and communicate meanings. Generally in adolescence a new capacity for synthesis of meanings and of images of self arise, making possible (and necessary) a new quality of *personal* relationship with God and others. And so on.[7]

In correlation with structural-developmental theories of faith, psychosocial theories give the practical theology of formation rich accounts of the predictable points of growth and struggle at which faith's foundations may be tested, deepened, or reworked.

In pointing in the direction of faith development theory I have in mind a broader range of resources than just my own work, though I consider it to be important. Among the growing number of vital contributions to faith development theory are: the work of James Loder on negation and transformation in faith; the psychoanalytic accounts of the formation of God representations, and of the dynamics of growth and recapitulation in faith offered by Ana-Marie Rizzuto and William Meisner, S.J., respectively; and the work of Don Browning on moral and religious development across the life cycle.[8] I think it is fair to say that faith development theory, in this broader sense, can be seen as an addition to fundamental theology inspired not so much by systematic as by practical theological concerns.

As practical theology appropriates the work of theories of faith development it contributes to our overcoming of static images of faith. In an era in which people *feel* reality as process, it is of signal importance that we have epistemologies of faith that help to clarify the relativities of our experiences of growth and change. Paradoxically, to take seriously the developmental relativity of growth and change in faith helps us to escape from the pervasive *relativism* that commends itself when we have no way of accounting for the dynamic but patterned processes of change by which we form and transform our ways of seeing and being in the world.

Now I turn to the third constituent element needed in a practical theology of Christian formation. Faith development theory illumines the dynamics, the structuring patterns, and the directions of transformation in faith viewed as a *generic* feature of human being and becoming. Its categories are formal and appropriate for a variety of particular content orientations in faith. But what, we must ask, are the distinctive characteristics of *Christian* faith? What qualities of personality, what strengths of character, what dispositional emotions are the fruits of loving and committing one's life to God in Christ? A practical theology of Christian formation needs a *theory of the virtues and affections of the Christian life*. It is important that such a theory not be so prescriptive about the particular behavioral expressions of faith that it becomes a new legalism. That would be to deny the fundamental qualities of freedom, responsibility, creativity, spontaneity, and joy that are the fruits of God's liberating and redemptive work in and through Jesus the Christ. Yet, in approaches to Christian formation informed by neoorthodox theologies there has been a notable lack of any adequate account of the virtues and gracious affections that give form and tensile strength to the life lived in joyful fealty to the sovereign love of God.

Communities of Christian faith need to rediscover lively images of the theological virtues of faith, hope, and love. In an era where we are promised instant gratification or immediate relief from pain, and where experiences are measured by the "highs" they bring, we need patient teaching and embodiment of the *steadfastness* and suspicion of volatile emotions involved in forming the Christian theological virtues. We need theological teachers who can lead Christians into the deeper foundations of the Christian life in the Holy Fear and love of God; in Gratitude, Repentance, Suffering, and Joy; and in the love of neighbor.

Can these virtues be taught? Can the gracious affections, those deep-going emotions that guide and animate the Christian's initiatives and responses in life, be learned? What qualities of community life, of prayer and spiritual direction, and of precept and example create the most fertile soil for growth of the genuine gifts of the spirit?

In a remarkable trilogy called *Free and Faithful in Christ,*[9] Jesuit moral theologian Bernard Häring is in the process of renewing that tradition in Christian ethics that teaches about the theological and eschatological virtues. Linking them to contemporary exegesis and theologies of the liberating work of Christ, and of responsibility as the creative discernment and constructive response of Christian persons and groups in history, Häring is revivifying our understanding of the patterns of Christian character.

Placing emphasis on the power of the gospel as narrative to give shape to Christian character, Stanley Hauerwas, like his teacher James Gustafson, is helping us toward fresh apprehensions of the *gestalt* of virtues that are the work of grace.[10] Finally, in *The Soul in Paraphrase,*[11] which reflects the influences of Paul Holmer, C. S. Lewis, and Jonathan Edwards, as well as the older and longer tradition of Catholic spiritual and sacramental theology, Don Saliers has given us a profound primer on the formation of Christian emotions through prayer and liturgy, with a refreshing freedom from dependence on modern psychology.

The fourth and last constituent element needed for a practical theology of Christian formation is *a theory of methodological principles and strategies for formation in faith.* In ways that are responsive and congruent with all of the three previous constituent elements, principles that guide in the design and selection of resources and in the shaping of specific educational ministries must be marshaled. In the absence of such principles the church's praxis of Christian formation will be confused, haphazard, piecemeal, and perhaps inherently self-contradictory. As we consider this fourth constituent element I find myself impressed again by how practical theology properly aims at leading us toward a *practical knowing,* a kind of "know-how" that is not merely technique or the result of imitation or pragmatic experimentation. Rather, as Rod Hunter is teaching us, *practical knowing* means the bringing together of our well-formed convictions about the purpose of an activity, our reflective experience and understanding of the persons and situations involved, our grasp of the shape of personal appropriations we desire to sponsor in the activity, all uniting to inform the selection or creation of specific strategies that are "fitting" and efficacious.

Formation occurs in the context of relationships. Truth in faith is incarnate, enacted. Education that is Christian is born of love—God's love for us in Christ, our love for others generated by Christ in us. No approach to Christian formation can put more than peripheral confidence in "teacher-proof" curricular resources. Programmed instruction will at best be but an educational game, informative and entertaining, but mainly supplemental. We are called into selfhood by others. We are called into Christian personhood by God through his Spirit and through the giving and demanding love of persons. At each stage of our growth in faith we require the dialogue of sponsorship, the nurture of a knowledgeable love.

A praxis approach to method and strategy in Christian formation stresses that faith is something we do. It is something we are. Faith is response to the sovereign love of God by embracing—at the most advanced level we can—our partnership in God's ongoing work of Creation, Governance, and Redemption/ Liberation. Christian community has at the heart of its concern the discernment and calling forth of each person's gifts. By discerning and calling forth gifts we help each other to find the *present* shape of our *vocation,* the life structure, for now, through which to realize full humanity by offering it in league with some aspect of God's work.

Method and strategy in Christian formation must take account of the imperative of ongoing *metanoia* ("repentance") and the invitation to ongoing growth. Communities of faith become defensive, idolatrous, and closed-ended when they settle for some one particular image of adult faith as adequate, expected, or final. Ecclesial communities that have no climate of developmental expectation collude with one of the aspects of original sin, namely, the refusal to grow—the effort to evade or avoid the pain of growth.

Finally, method and strategy in Christian formation takes seriously that most valuable of all commodities, time. Growth takes time; relationships take time; prayer, praise, and proclamation take time; planning and action for service and liberation take time. A practical theology of Christian formation must use time for all it makes possible—insist upon it, covenant for it, and "enjoy" it fully. By the same token it will honor time, guard the quality of its spending, and work faithfully at its stewardship.

Now by way of summary and recapitulation, we have identified and briefly characterized four constituent elements of a practical theology of Christian formation. They are:

1. A theory of the sovereign love of God as the pattern of action underlying and giving character to the cosmic process.
2. A theory of development in faith.
3. A theory of the virtues and affections of the Christian life.
4. A theory of methodological principles and strategies for formation in faith.

I hope that this effort toward beginning to marshal a coherent approach to these four needed constituent elements of a practical theology of Christian formation proves to be helpful. There may be more lasting value in the identification of the four needed constituent elements themselves than in my own particular efforts to sketch the program.

Conclusion

In concluding, I want to focus a few issues regarding method and primary audience in practical theology. These issues are raised for us by the traditions of empirical and process theology which have flourished at the Divinity School of the University of Chicago. Currently they issue from the concerns for pluralism, for a public language, and for the philosophical foundations of theological work—including practical theology—which are expressed by David Tracy, Don Browning, and others in the field of this discussion.

In chapter 10 of this volume ("Pastoral Theology in a Pluralistic Age") Browning extends his important concern for the recovery of normative perspectives in pastoral care. In this chapter he characterizes the context of religious (and nonreligious) pluralism in which pastoral theologians find themselves working. He focuses for us the challenge of addressing ethical and moral issues with coherent normative perspectives that can be shared and justified to persons and groups who do not share Christian commitments. Resonant with the work of David Tracy, which has deeply influenced his own, Browning develops four theses that strike a balance between confessional theological allegiance and the need for accountability in publicly accessible, philosophical categories (pp. 187–202).

I am grateful for Browning's leadership toward the recovery of normative foundations in pastoral care. I am glad that he integrally relates his way of formulating normative principles both to Jewish and Christian roots, and to theories of the life cycle. I share with him the conviction that our expressions of moral concern and efforts at ethical guidance must be publicly intelligible and rationally explicated and, when necessary, rationally defended.

In addressing the foundations of a practical theology of formation I do not wish to ignore either the concerns about pluralism or the significance of a public language and rational foundation for accounting for the convictions, goals, and methods of Christian nurture. Two factors, however, lead me to stress more the ecclesial character of practical theology in general, and of a theology of education in particular, than does Browning.

First, *formation* in faith may and should prepare one for fruitful contributions in a pluralistic society. But if effective, formation in faith means formation in relation to the centers of value, the images of power, the rituals, and the normative stories *of a particular community.* It is my considered conviction that exclusivistic interpretations of Christology and of Christian faith are inherently self-contradictory.[12] At its heart, I believe, Christian faith calls persons to ways of seeing and being in the world that represent the fulfillment of what it means to be human. In ways that have integrity and reason when examined from the standpoint of other human perspectives, Christian faith sponsors growth toward full humanity. But it does not do so without the provision of profound experiences of solidarity with a worshiping, proclaiming, teaching, and missional community.

Second, our commitment to honoring pluralism may mean biting our tongue when, by heritage and vocation, we have access to something in the richness of Christian faith and the power of God that can *really* help. There is a vast hunger and deep need for perspectives on life that have the power to "go all the way." By this I mean that people sense deep down somewhere that the glitter of secularization, the distractions of the media, and the hypnotic engagement in consumption are but canvas skins covering yawning abysses in our lives. Academic theologians and conventional church people may fail to see how powerful theistic imagery and religious rhetoric and vision are in our era. People want to know the whither and whence of our lives. Consciously or unconsciously they long for a plumb line in relation to which things in their lives can be righted and ordered. In the uncertainties and anxieties of our complex, dangerous world, people long for eyes to see and for hearts to respond to the moving shape of One who is our author and destiny. There is a danger in identifying practical theology with the ethical, at the expense of a Holy Awe before the *Mysterium Tremendum.* In our concern for public language and for rational foundations for our theologies let us not underestimate the archetypal and historical power of cross and resurrection, the universal longing for messiah, and the deep rationality of our response, in kind, to a universal love.

NOTES

1. David Tracy, *Blessed Rage for Order: The New Pluralism in Theology* (New York: Seabury, 1975); *The Analogical Imagination* (New York: Seabury, Crossroad Books, 1981). Jürgen Habermas, *Theory and Practice* (Bos-

ton: Beacon Press, 1973). Richard J. Bernstein, *Praxis and Action* (Philadelphia: University of Pennsylvania Press, 1971).

2. Edward Farley's contribution to this volume, Chapter 2, documents this process suggestively.

3. My colleague at Emory University, Rodney Hunger, is doing some helpful fundamental thinking about the practical knowing of pastoral care and ministry. I acknowledge my indebtedness to his as yet unpublished ideas here.

4. Cf. Wolfhart Pannenberg, *Theology and the Kingdom of God* (Philadelphia: Westminster, 1969), especially chap. 4.

5. I have treated this tri-metaphorical doctrine of God at length in *To See the Kingdom: The Theological Vision of H. Richard Niebuhr* (Nashville, TN: Abingdon, 1974), chap. 4

6. Tracy, *Blessed Rage for Order,* pp. 181 ff.

7. See James W. Fowler, *Stages of Faith* (San Francisco: Harper & Row, 1981). Also, Fowler, "Future Christians and Church Education," in Theodore Runyon, ed., *Hope for the Church* (Nashville, TN: Abingdon, 1980). For a brilliant extension of Piaget's theory of cognitive growth in the direction of an account of personality development, see Robert Kegan, *The Evolving Self* (Cambridge, MA: Harvard University Press, 1982).

8. James E. Loder, *The Transforming Moment* (San Francisco: Harper & Row, 1981). Ana-Marie Rizzuto, *The Birth of the Living God* (Chicago: University of Chicago Press, 1979). William Meissner, "Psychoanalysis and Religion," *Journal of Psychoanalysis* (1978). Don Browning, *Generative Man* (Philadelphia: Westminster, 1973).

9. Bernard Häring, *Free and Faithful in Christ* (New York: Seabury, Crossroad Books, 1978).

10. Most recently in Stanley Hauerwas, *A Community of Character* (Notre Dame, IN: University of Notre Dame Press, 1981), especially chap. 7.

11. Don Saliers, *The Soul in Paraphrase* (New York: Seabury, Crossroad Books, 1980).

12. I find helpful support for this position in John Cobb, *Christ in a Pluralistic Age* (Philadelphia: Westminster, 1975).

9. Practical Theology and Pastoral Care: An Essay in Pastoral Theology

JAMES N. LAPSLEY

MY TASK here is to deal focally with one subdiscipline in practical theology—the one that has to do with the various activities of ministry collectively called pastoral care, that discipline we call pastoral theology. Since I believe that this is the best thing to call the discipline that deals focally with pastoral care, I shall mainly be trying in this chapter to show how pastoral theology is an integral theological discipline in responsible relationship to what are sometimes called the traditional disciplines of theology, and how it may contribute to the illumination of both the coherence and the tension among the several subdisciplines of practical theology. The question of coherence and tension will be discussed only in the relation between pastoral theology and Christian ethics, although I hope that some indirect light may be shed on some of the other subdisciplines represented in this volume, as well as some not represented, such as church administration.

History as Advantage and Burden

Of the several areas of practical theology, pastoral care is the only one with a history of an associated discipline carrying the word "theology."[1] Pastoral theology has been a part of the conceptual apparatus of the churches for at least 232 years.[2] It has been taught as such in the school where I teach for at least 160 years.[3] I shall not attempt to rehearse here all the meanings that pastoral theology has had during the last two centuries.[4] With one or two exceptions they all affirm that it is of the essence of the church and its ministry to direct a concern toward the personal dimensions of the lives of its members. There was much confusion—a confusion that persists in some quarters until the present—about what acts of ministry might best be termed pastoral. Some writers held that only a relatively few acts, those focused upon the particular needs of individuals and usually called pastoral care, were the proper subject of pastoral theology. Others, and they have been in the majority, have held that most acts of ministry, with the possible exception of those involved directly in preaching, were the domain of pastoral theology.

In my judgment this confusion is due in no small measure to an inherent ambiguity in the term "pastoral" stemming from its origin in the shepherd metaphor as it was used in the Bible. The term is associated with the intensely personal and unique, as in Psalm 23 and as in the parable of the one lost sheep in Matthew 18, but also often with the protective, guiding, and providing functions of the shepherd with the whole flock. The latter implies church discipline as a part of the care of the flock, and John T. McNeill has shown us how the churches have alternated, and sometimes vacillated, between these two poles of meaning throughout much of their history, as they addressed in practice the question of how the one and the many are related.[5]

The principal advantage of the history of pastoral theology is the insistence of the churches that what is pastoral is also inherently theological. That is, despite occasional aberrations in direction of mere "hints and helps," especially in the early twentieth century, the churches have viewed the *actual* (as opposed to the ideal) *personal and/or spiritual state of affairs* of individuals and groups of Christians as being of importance theologically.

The burden of the history is its ambiguity and resultant confusion about whether pastoral refers only or mainly to acts of pastoral care performed in relation to individuals and small groups, or whether, for example, a minister's protest against local television programming in the interest of protecting his or her flock may also be pastoral in intent. It is my position that any view of pastoral theology must accept, at least in principle, this burden of ambiguity. For both poles of the ambiguity, the individual and the whole flock, are themselves so closely related that the shepherd cannot afford to attend to one and not the other.

Seward Hiltner saw that the pastoral care acts of the suffering individual and the many other acts of ministry performed by the "pastor" must both be taken into account in a responsible pastoral theology. In his landmark work, *Preface to Pastoral Theology,* he devised a perspectival model in part to take the ambiguity into account.[6] Hiltner also pointed out, of course, that even in one single act of ministry no one perspective is necessarily always dominant. He held that the other two cognate perspectives as he defined them—communicating and organizing—were also present in principle in every act of ministry and might at some points become dominant even in what seemed to be an act of pastoral care addressed to personal need. For our purposes here it is important also to note that Hiltner was the first writer about pastoral theology to insist in a sustained and systematic way that studying the data of ministry from the shepherding perspective, which meant among other things that the minister had some theological questions in mind, could yield constructive contributions to other branches of theology.

A Constructive Proposal

In 1969 I defined *pastoral theology* as "the study of all aspects of the care of persons in the church in a context of theological inquiry, including implications for other branches of theology."[7] In 1977 this definition was reiterated,[8] and I find no compelling reason to change it now, even though I do not contend that it might not be improved in some respects. In the definition the *purposes* of the study of all aspects of the care of persons are not in focus, and one of them, the main one still, in the eyes of many, is implied rather than stated at all. This purpose is that of guiding and improving the care of persons. It is this purpose that Rodney Hunter took as his theme when surveying the results of the Pastoral Theology Colloquy in Honor of Seward Hiltner held at Princeton in March 1980. Hunter asserted that a serious flaw in the development of pastoral theology as a distinct discipline lies in its character as a practical knowledge or wisdom that lacks both academic status and a tradition in Western epistemology. He held that such knowledge can only in part be derived from normative disciplines, whether they be theological or scientific disciplines, and that it must be developed also by pragmatic means, that is, by trial and error.[9] All this is a very complex process, as Hunter also noted, and complexity accounts in part for our lack of a large body of "assured results" in pastoral theology. I shall return to Hunter's question in the final part of the chapter.

The central characteristic of any theory of pastoral care must be the discernment of and appropriate strategies and tactics for attaining the *possibilities* for a particular person or persons as these are understood within a model of human life that is responsibly related to an identifiable position in Christian theology. It is this emphasis upon the *possibilities,* and hence, also, *limits,* for particular persons that gives pastoral theology its peculiar identity among theological disciplines. It is also this emphasis that provides its distinction from ethics. Pastoral theology is not a branch of ethics, as Don Browning urges,[10] because ethics is focused upon norms and goals as its primary concern, and because much pastoral care is only tangentially related to ethics in any developed sense of that term. Rather the "cup of cold water" extended in a personal relationship is generic to the gospel itself. To be sure, ethical and even disciplinary questions do explicitly arise in pastoral care (the latter when there is a "clear and present danger" to self or others), but in these instances the theologically discerned possibilities retain status as criteria.

The other purpose of pastoral theology is found in its "implications for other branches of theology." These implications may be for "the identifiable position in Christian theology" to which a particular pastoral theologian may be primarily related, they may be for another branch or branches of practical theology, or they may be for issues that permeate many positions and branches of theology. The function of a "theological position" in pastoral theology is that of providing discipline and coherence to study. The articulation of such a position provides for the revelation of assumptions and for the basic principles of method—for every position entails methodological assumptions as well as those related to content and may preclude some kinds of procedures. Procedures related to the use of ancillary disciplines, such as psychology and sociology, are, of course, of particular importance in pastoral theology. The assertion of a particular theological position in relation to pastoral theology does not involve a final commitment to that position, since such commitment can be made by a Christian, in my view, only to the gospel itself. Indeed, pastoral theology sometimes results in a shift in theological models by its practitioners.

The question of where one *begins* in pastoral theology must be answered phenomenologically. One begins where one is—whether with a suffering person or a general issue that is discerned as important. Wherever one begins, however, all the elements will become dialectically involved as study proceeds. In practice this dialectic does not follow, always, a specifiable sequence, but rather is subject to individual style and varying circumstances. One does not, for instance, always begin with a theological question. The beginning point may be an issue in a particular case of pastoral care, or an issue that seems to pervade many such cases. It may even be a public issue, such as the question of changes in character structure in the culture, that is the beginning point. But in every instance there must be some kind of scrutiny of data arising from the effort of the ministry of the church—clerical or lay—to assist some person or persons within a relationship to them. It is this grubbing in the root systems of human need and human hope with the intent to strengthen, nurture, and if possible, to aid development that provides the particularity of pastoral theology, and it is the source of its potential and actual contributions to theology.

My own approach to pastoral theology has for some time been through a certain kind of process theology. It is becoming clearer that it is a kind of Reformed process theology, as contrasted with the more Arminian-Wesleyan version of much of the literature. A general interlocking model for integrating human concerns and possibilities, as well as limits, with theological constructs was first elaborated in *Salvation and Health: The Interlocking Processes of Life*.[11]

The model developed in *Salvation and Health* to depict the relationship between the processes of salvation and health in persons is also a model of the person in relationship. The terms "salvation" and "health" may be understood to point to the goals of human life employed on the one hand in theology and on the other in the human sciences. The processes indicated by these terms do not occur apart from one another, although they may be analyzed separately by abstracting them from the concrete matrix of human and transhuman events. They are, rather, interlocking in character, varying according to the dynamics of the three factors in the relationship between them: *development, maintenance,* and *participation.*

By *development* is meant the differentiating and integrating qualities of an organism, both as to structure and to function. Differentiation and reintegration are most striking in embryos and infants, but they recur obviously through adolescence and then more subtly, at least functionally, throughout life, or most of it. Development may or may not include growth, an increase in size, even though "growth" is commonly used in both theology and psychology to mean development. The basic developmental model is biological, but for some time development has been regarded as also occurring in the psyche and the person as a whole throughout much of life by such theorists as Erikson and Loevenger.[12]

Maintenance refers to the relatively stable equilibrium needed by the person, as organism, to survive. Organisms can tolerate instability only within limits, as Cannon, who introduced the term *homeostasis* to denote this principle, established.[13] This concept has been modified to incorporate relatively more instability within stability since Cannon's work, but the principle remains as a primary characteristic of organisms, including human organisms. In the realm of the psyche the most prominent factors related to maintenance needs are a sense of personal identity and a sense of self worth, without which persons cannot function as persons. Development itself, as well as many kinds of attitudes and activities, may often serve the purpose of maintenance. When this occurs, it may be called a *compensation.* Something in the spheres of identity or sense of worth, or in both, is felt to be lacking or threatened. Much human behavior is primarily compensatory in this sense, and some, although not completely due to felt deficits or threats, has a compensatory component or components. Since the twin factors of identity and self worth do not always lead the individual in the same direction, a further complexity of conflict is often a part of the struggle to relate appropriately to the world.

Participation refers to the interaction of the individual with the lives of others and with the world. Participation in its receptive mode is a necessity of all human life and undergirds both development and maintenance. In its contributory and mutual modes it is a part of all lives being lived beyond the level of barest maintenance. Although not all participation is constructive, among the possibilities for participation is that which we may call salvatory, in that it contributes to the enhancement and preservation of the values actualized in a human life and toward the possibilities for the actualization and enhancement in the lives of others and their preservation. Such salvatory participation makes also a contribution to the life of God. For God is participating already in the lives of human beings, guiding and persuading them toward a vision of harmony, peace, and love. They in turn, through the actualization of these values in their unique personhood, return to God a novel enrichment, contributing to the development of the divine life. Divine initiative and grace, as powerfully reflected in the story of the exodus from Egypt and in the impact of Jesus Christ upon human personal and cultural history undergrid all human salvatory participation, transmuting the essential tragic character of human life into a divine comedy.

Important for the use of this model is the way in which the factors interact with one another to produce six levels of human functioning. These levels ascend from *one* to *six* according to the degree of salvatory participation possible within a given level. That is, the criterion employed to establish the ranking of levels is a theological one focusing upon salvatory potential, even though each level contains also health components that do not always correspond in degree of health to the degree of salvatory potential. There is, thus, no one-to-one correspondence between salvation and health. Health is viewed as a basic potential for human functioning that affords a greater or lesser degree of possibility for salvatory participation.

In the case presented in the following pages levels three and four are those most directly involved. So I shall only sketch the other levels very briefly while placing levels three and four in context with the model.

Level one is characterized by a struggle of the human organism to *maintain* life, and most energy is directed toward this end. Salvatory participation is still present, however, in interaction with other persons, minimal though it may be. Newborns, the acutely ill, and the dying are primary examples of persons at this level. In *level two* development is the key factor, and the other two factors of maintenance and participation are to be understood as primarily serving developmental needs. "Normal" children and adolescents are persons whose participatory and maintenance functions serve as aids to development, and they are the ones we most frequently find at this level, although adults who radically shift directions in their lives may be also thus characterized.

At *level three* the dominant feature is the organization of life around maintenance needs. Development and participation function mainly to aid the person in keeping his or her psychic and somatic balance. They thus play primarily a compensating role. Balance is felt or perceived both consciously and unconsciously, and a high value is usually placed on stability, although sometimes behaviors regarded as unstable by others (and even by the persons engaging in them) appear in the service of maintenance of balance. Identity and worth are protected or recovered by such endeavors, but more often small compensatory shifts in patterns of participation are made, or less spectacular development of skills and attitude occurs to guard them. Even so, their participation exercises a great influence on the lives of others because of their great numbers and the general regularity and dependability of it. Upon the relatively benign effects, as opposed to the destructive effects, of this kind of participation the stability and, to some extent, the development of society depends. But compensatory participation is also the source of prejudice and other anxiety-laden behavior that can contribute to the destruction of culture in time of crisis. Hence, compensated maintenance patterns are ambiguous in their impact. Their salvatory effects are often only a happy by-product of their principal function of keeping individuals on a relatively even keel.

The distinctive characteristic of *level four* is participation over rather long periods of time that is in the service of development, but that usually also contributes significantly to the lives of others and to the institutional structures of society. Persons at level four are most apt to be young adults embarking on marriages and careers, although in the changing patterns of our present culture they may be older adults making second or third (or even more) essays in the spheres of either love or work or both. Initially, both marriage and vocation serve primarily developmental needs associated with intimacy and procreation on the one hand and identity as an adult with associated achievement orientations on the other. Although the direction of heterosexual relational patterns is far from clear, it does seem clear that the developmental character of them will be increasingly recognized. Vocational motivation usually undergoes a shift after a time, resulting in long-term commitment to the same vocation, if the person is not "caught" in it, or change to another.

At *level five* participation is primarily in the service of enhancing accurately perceived values in human life and culture—both in the life of the person whose participation it is and in the lives of others. Relatively greater freedom from maintenance and developmental needs is a basis of more accurate perception and strength for action. *Level six* represents a further increase in potential for salvatory participation to an ideal degree represented in depictions of Jesus Christ as capable of very great freedom of choice and the power to take the most salvatory path—in his case a self-sacrificial one.

The idea of *spirit* will be used as a focal integrating concept by means of which I shall relate the interlocking model directly to pastoral care and concerns. Although the notion of spirit has had a long and multifarious career in theology and philosophy, I believe it is legitimate to use it in a sense close to its original meaning of "breath" or "wind"—a dynamic energy characterizing life. The human spirit may be at least provisionally defined as the intensity and direction of human life, or more specifically that perspective on persons that brings intensity and direction into focus, as contrasted with psyche, which may be viewed as the person's *structure* of internal relations, that is, that perspective bringing the structural motifs into focus, as in the structural model of psychoanalysis comprised of id, ego, and superego. The spirit cannot be separated from the psyche, nor can either be separated from the body. Rather each has validity as a perspective on the human being.[14]

The human spirit may be understood as having three vectors. The term vector, borrowed from physics, denotes a direction of some magnitude of energy. Vector may be contrasted with scalar, a point on a scale or "ladder" without magnitude or direction. Vectors of spirit represent divergent movements within a life at a given time. These directions may or may not be collisional or convergent. The three vectors of the spirit that I find in persons are vectors on the self, other persons, and vocation. I shall not attempt to define these terms at this point, but I believe they will become clearer in the discussion of the case presented below.

One final concept is needed to connect psyche with spirit. This is *vision,* the affect-laden images within the psyche that supply motivational power to the spirit. Here I am following the general line of thinking developed by Silvan Tomkins in his work on the affects. Although emphasizing affects, particularly as mediators of the drives, Tomkins was also aware of the diversity of the sources of powerful imagery in comprising what he termed the "image of an end state to be achieved . . . compounded of diverse sensory, affective and memory imagery or any combination or transformation of these."[15] Here the psyche impinges upon the spirit, providing guidance and energy, but also inhibition and sometimes confusion of direction.

Vectors of the Spirit in the Case of "Beth"

Without attempting to deal with all aspects of the theoretical model outlined above, I offer the following case as an example of how the three-vector concept of spirit may illumine the theory of the pastoral care dimension of pastoral theology, and how it may help to address the question of the relation between pastoral theology and other branches of theology, in particular, ethics.

The following instance of pastoral care was reported by a young woman minister whose name is Jean:

> Beth is an adult in the church. I have come to know her quite personally through a small prayer group of which we are members

along with several other married couples. Beth is a sincere, outspoken person who is not likely to hide her faults; she is very open about herself to those she knows. She is generally happy, well adjusted, and particularly concerned about her Christian growth—she works at it constantly, almost in an immature way (in that she does not understand that one does not "work" at her faith as much as try to live within the grace already given by profession of faith).

I had intended to talk to Beth privately about something she shared in the prayer group three weeks ago, but something always seemed to prevent it until yesterday, when I called her and asked if she had some free time to chat with me. She responded warmly and enthusiastically and told me to come right over.

The problem that Beth had brought before the prayer group and that I wanted to discuss with her had to do with a neighborhood woman who had called her and asked her if she would let her join the neighborhood car pool. The woman had a five-year-old child and no car. Beth had refused on the grounds that she had heard by the grapevine that this woman was a very undesirable person to be involved with and that she was a clinger. Beth pointed out that the woman was so desperate that she even offered to pay Beth to take her child. I felt very burdened with this situation and hoped that by talking to Beth I might be able to get her to see this woman as a ministry—which she is always looking for, anyway.

I arrived at Beth's and we commented on the weather, her small daughter being home, and the fact that we would probably be interrupted frequently.

Minister, picking up book on table (1): Oh, are you an Oswald Chambers [writer of devotional books based upon biblical texts] fan?

Beth (1): Yes, I think he's so terrific. I always feel he speaks right to me, he knows what I've been thinking about all day.

Minister (2): I sure do appreciate him. I even used one of his pages to lead off the meeting of the college group I did last week.

Beth (2): Yes, that's right. Bill [her husband] did mention you had done such a good job.

Minister (3): I used this one on the call of Isaiah, the idea that God doesn't compel you to do something, but rather he calls everyone and those who hear and are ready, answer.

Beth (3): But Jean, I think he does call us. Why sometimes I've felt his hand on me just pushing me to do something [Beth uses hand gestures here to emphasize].

Minister (4): Yes, well that may be true in certain situations, but I meant more in terms of what you do with your life.

Beth (4): That's true, so many factors go into what you become. I feel very definitely that my background has had a lot to do with the person I have turned out to be. You know, don't you, that both my parents were deaf mutes?

Minister (5): Sally had told me, but I'd be interested in how you see this situation to have influenced you, Beth.

Beth (5): Well, my parents had such a different outlook on life. They always felt so inadequate in everything; they had such an inferiority complex and this naturally affected the way I feel about life.

Minister (6): You feel inadequate in some ways?

Beth (6): Yes [emphatically]! I have a terrible lack of self-confidence—although some people may think I have too much—like, in my Sunday School teaching.

Minister (7): You lack self-confidence in your teaching?

Beth (7): Yes, and I just need something to bolster me up and keep me going all the time.

Minister (8): And you feel your faith does this for you?

Beth (8): Oh, yes, I just couldn't do all I'm doing with those kids without it. And I'm just growing so much. But now that's enough about me. You certainly didn't come over here to talk about me. What did you want to talk about, or wasn't there anything special?

Minister (9): Well, Beth, ever since that night when you mentioned the neighborhood lady who wanted to get into your car pool, I've been burdened about this woman, and I wondered if you had any more contact with her or heard anything about her?

Beth, looking very worried, a little surprised and flustered (9): Oh, no, I haven't heard anything. That was such a pitiful thing, that woman. I just felt so sorry for her, Jean, and I felt so bad about turning her down like that. But here was this strange woman calling me up—I didn't even know her—asking me to be in our car pool when she didn't even have a car . . .

Minister (10): You felt imposed upon?

Beth (10): Yes, and besides, I knew already that the others didn't want her in the car pool.

Minister (11): You felt then that refusing her was a responsible action toward the rest of the members of the car pool?

Beth (11): Yes, why I had even heard them talking about it as early as last August, about how we had to get the car pool filled up in a hurry so she couldn't get in. And I said to the organizer even then, "Why, how can you, as a Christian, justify such an attitude?" But then I just went along with her. After I talked to the woman on the phone I cried, I felt so bad about it. But I thought about it and talked about it—and I know it was just selfish of me—but I felt that if I got involved, the next thing I knew it would be, "Take me to the grocery store, and take me shopping," and well, I have my own life to lead.

Minister (12): You felt that she would impose on you further?

Beth (12): Yes, and besides, it might have been different if I had known her at all and could empathize with her, but I only knew her by one very embarrassing phone call.

Minister (13): It would have been different if you had known her personally?

Beth (13): Yes, of course. I still feel so guilty about it, Jean. Ever since she called I haven't been able to stop thinking about it, and that was last fall.

Minister (14): Oh, I didn't know that.

Beth (14): Yes, and the only thing I could have done was to drop out of the car pool I was in and drive this woman's child to school every day, and well, I was just too selfish to do this, I guess.

Minister (15): You felt this was too much to expect of you?

Beth (15): Yes, I certainly did. Besides, lots of children walk to school.

Minister (16): You didn't feel it was a very important matter to be concerned with?

Beth (16): Well, of course, these are all rationalizations, I know, to justify what I did, and I still feel bad about it, which is why I brought it up in the prayer group . . .

Minister (17): She pushed herself on you?

Beth, wanting to end the conversation (17): Yes, well, I don't know; as I said before, if I had known her personally, it might have been different. You just don't know how to handle those situations, and anyway, I feel if God had really meant me to help her, he would have given me another chance.

From here I decided she really did not want to pursue the discussion, so to relieve the tension that had built up because of her guilt, I brought up a similar situation I am involved in and have been unable to do something constructive in for two years. . . .

The vector of the spirit on the self is very evident and very intense in Beth. She tells us of her efforts to "grow," and her low self-esteem and how this needs rather continual bolstering (Beth, 7). Later in the conversation we learn that she feels that she needs to protect herself from being exploited by the importunate telephoner, and especially from being rejected by her peers in the car pool. At the same time we learn that she seeks to be open in her relationships, that she is said to be generally happy, and that the burden of guilt she bears because of the rejection of the would-be car pooler is said to be a somewhat isolated segment of her self-vector.

Her vector of spirit toward other people is also prominent in the conversation. Her parents, God, the would-be car pooler, her peer group, and her daughter and husband are all mentioned, and her relationship with Jean, the minister, is also clearly playing a role. The deaf mute parents may be dead, since they are referred to in the past tense, but obviously still alive in what Silvan Tomkins called "the Image" of Beth's psyche. In her *vision* God is a pusher, a somewhat unusual role for God, who is more likely a puller, caller, or summoner, suggesting that her God may also be a deaf mute, among other attributes. The would-be car pooler stands in the role of the indirect object of the accusing conscience, the car pool people are in the primary relational network of approval and belonging, and Jean, the minister, seems to be a supportive identification (perhaps overidentification) figure.

Beth's vocational vector is not explicitly in focus, but forms the context of the conflict. Being a mother is obviously of central importance, and the subvector of being neighbor seems to be in conflict with it, as well as with the peer support group. God, the pusher, relentlessly points toward the neighbor. We may assume, I think, that Beth also has a vocation as wife, but this is muted in the conversation. Other elements are a matter of sheer conjecture and may be absent.

We can only see glimpses of Beth's vision. The element of the parents as well intentioned but weak victimizers is there, and God as a stronger, perhaps, but not, certainly, omnipotent version of the parents is present in consciousness. The vectors of the spirit are thus shaped by the generating vision in interaction with the phenomenal world. In Beth's case the persons mentioned above and the symbols of her vocation of mother, as these are found in the culture, are the prominent aspects of that world.

Coherence and Tension Between Pastoral Theology and Ethics

The issue of the relation of pastoral theology to Christian ethics is seen in the case in the struggle between the *possibilities* perceived by Beth and by Jean and the *norm* of being neighbor. Here I may say that I affirm Jean's concern with possibilities, but I think that she was too limited in her vision of them, and too inclined to protect Beth from confronting her own distress about this matter (Minister 15, 17). Beth is paying a high price for her passive-aggressive stance toward this "neighbor," and there is a genuine moral question there, also. To insist simply that Beth meet the norm and call the "neighbor" would be probably even worse, since that would simply abandon *possibility* for *standards,* the moralizing for which the churches have been rightly indicted by the pastoral care movement, among other critics.

However, the distress in Beth's life clearly needs more attention, and the whole question of some kind of responsible approach to the "neighbor" needs exploring. We do not know that her primary need is for a place in the car pool. That appears to be the signal, but what it signifies we do not know. Clearly, some risks may have to be taken to find the possibilities, not only in the ethical sphere but in others. Pastoral theology posits that trust in relationship enables appropriate risks to be taken. Ethics, on the other hand, needs always to keep the norm in mind, whatever it discerns it to be, but it needs also to attend to the particularities of possibility as these can emerge in pastoral relationships.

Viewed now in the context of our larger question of the relationship between pastoral theology and ethics, we can see some features of the theory of pastoral care which are of particular interest. In the general framework of the interlocking model, Beth seems to be, at first glance, functioning at level four. This means that she is engaging in the kinds of developmental behavior appropriate for a young adult, and that these behaviors serve to a significant degree participatory ends, seen in her role as mother and Sunday School teacher, and glimpsed in her relationship to her husband. Maintenance functions, whether biological, psychological, or social, do not seem to be an obtrusive part of her life.

But, as we become better acquainted with her, we begin to wonder if the guilty conscience focused on one phone call is not so isolated a phenomenon in her life as first appeared. We find that she is struggling to maintain her self-esteem in her teaching and in her peer group, toward which she had an attitude more appropriate for mid-adolescence than for a young adult. She seems to have an image of God related rather directly to early childhood experience. These considerations lead me to question whether she is best understood as functioning at level four, or, if she is, whether she is barely hanging on to it. A slide toward more evident level-three behavior seems a real possibility, that is, toward a level of functioning in which both developmental and participatory functions serve maintenance needs of self-esteem and identity in compensatory fashion.

The minister's focal problem, then, is that of deciding whether to try and strengthen her existing vision and behavior pattern as seen through the vectors of her spirit, perhaps in the process helping her to find a compromise between her guilty conscience and the need to maintain the esteem of her peers and whatever else may be comprehended under the phrase "my own life to lead," or whether to try to establish more firmly a level-four pattern of developmental participation through pastoral counseling over a period of time. If the latter approach is chosen and carried out, no one can say whether her sense of guilt would still produce anguish—which in turn might lead to constructive ethical action. The minister's hope would be that strengthened self-esteem would make fear of loss of peer group participation less a threat, and that constructive action in such matters as the telephone call for help could be taken in such fashion as to include both the needs of the caller and her vectors of vocation and self. That is, the vectors of the spirit would no longer be tangled and convoluted as they are now, but rather a clearer and more viable vision would inform all three vectors so that they are complementary though distinct, even though choices, sometimes hard choices, will still have to be made.

Some of the tension between ethics and pastoral theology can be seen rather clearly here. When someone has enough guilt that is directed at a seemingly appropriate object, as contrasted with one that is clearly inappropriate as in classical neuroticism, even if the guilt is thought to have its roots in distortion of vision, should the risk be taken that the energy directed toward the needs of others will still be there if the distortions are corrected? While there may well be other good reasons for Jean, the minister in this case, to hesitate before engaging in counseling toward the correction of such distortion—such as her own level of competence and Beth's readiness for "contract" counseling with this kind of goal—the ethical dimension itself must weigh in her decision as well.

In this case one ethical matter, which may, indeed, appear trivial to some, exemplifies some aspects of what has come to be regarded by many as an endemic conflict between pastoral care and ethics, especially social ethics. Does not guilt, not unlike that experienced by Beth, contribute mightily to the upbuilding of most of the world's eleemosynary institutions? Although I do not believe that all social action is necessarily based upon guilt, the most fundamental social reform in Western history, the abolition of human slavery, would never have been effected without it. So the question posed for the minister, Jean, in the case of "Beth" is far from trivial in its implications.

And yet to focus only on the tension and disjunction between pastoral theology and ethics would give a false picture of their relationship. We have already noted that ethics can learn something about actual possibilities and limits in human life from pastoral theology. It is fruitless to exhort the Beths of this world to love their neighbor unless one is also prepared to enter their anguished world and to help them discover their own possibilities. On the other hand pastoral theologians need to keep in mind that their pastoral care is always carried out with reference to some kind of norm of human conduct, and that the vision of life, and especially of the future, found guiding the spirits of persons embody some kinds of norms as well. Although ethical questions may or may not be in focus in pastoral care, they cannot be relegated to the final session of a long series in pastoral counseling, at least in the mind of the counselor.

Even in social ethics the relationship is not always disjunctive, and not ever as disjunctive as stereotyped arguments sometimes portray it. Many a pastor has found that, in order to help a person, a family must be helped, and in order to help the family a neighborhood must be helped, and in order for the neighborhood to be helped political pressure must be brought to bear.

In spite of these convergences it would be a mistake to try to include pastoral theology under the umbrella of ethics as a discipline. Pastoral theology must be free to focus upon possibilities in human life and the means for attaining them wîthout always asking the normative question as a prior commitment procedurally, which tends to obscure possibilities. Its convergences with ethics are no greater in principle than those that it has with other branches of theology, especially the other subdisciplines of practical theology.

Pastoral Theology as a Theological Discipline

Let us turn now to the final question with which we are concerned, that of the status of pastoral theology as a theological discipline and its possible contributions to the theological enterprise. First, I suggest that the interlocking model as a general theory of human functioning, with the three-vector concept of spirit capable of taking account of the idiosyncracies of individual personalities, does provide a theological mode of understanding human behavior, and especially pastoral care. As such, it can provide, in principle at least, a way of answering Rodney Hunter's question, to which I alluded earlier, about the nature of practical knowledge, understood now as practical theology. The most difficult part of the practical knowledge question is the responsible linking of the high-level abstract character of most theological thinking to the very low-level abstract thinking needed to understand the personal and the idiosyncratic.

In the case of "Beth" we find some rather idiosyncratic elements—deaf mute parents being the most obvious—but we also find some elements such as low self-esteem, a guilty conscience, motherhood, and Sunday School teaching that enable us to hypothesize how her functioning may be related to the general interlocking model through use of the three-vector conception of spirit. This in turn was shown to have significance for the decision making of the minister, who needs to choose on theological grounds what course to follow in her ministry to "Beth."

One general import for theology to be drawn from a case like this is, of course, the need for theologians to be careful of their abstractions. History records a significant number of theologians and theologically informed moralists who failed to take much account of particulars, such as Torquemada and Cromwell, and others, such as Augustine on human sexuality, who tended to generalize too much from their own experience without asking how general their experience actually was.

This latter point is also an important issue for the pastoral theologian, who must continually ask the question of how generalizable the knowledge gained from any instance of pastoral care may be. In the case of "Beth" we found that certain features of the case may be generalizable——those pertaining to guilt and its relation to archaic parental-divine images in her vision of the world, even though there are admittedly idiosyncratic features in that vision as well. This kind of generalization, even though congruent with other findings in dynamic psychology, has the status of an hypothesis subject to support or disconfirmation as theological knowledge. Such support or disconfirmation can come best through a coherent linking model of human functioning such as the interlocking model.

A more specific point suggested for theology by this case is that generalizations about human guilt are full of pitfalls. The theological understanding of guilt in the case is not necessarily in logical contradiction with itself, but it does point to the tragic character of existence in which every gain may also entail an important loss. It calls theology to a kind of cost accounting to which it has been for the most part unaccustomed, but with which, I believe, it needs to become more familiar.

In conclusion I want to emphasize that I do not set forth the model in this chapter as in any sense a final answer to the serious and deep problems that form the theme of this book, but I believe that it does show how some of the problems may be approached. I invite improvements from others, or the construction of entirely different linking models based upon convictions and assumptions they may hold.

NOTES

1. This tends to be true of Protestant traditions. Roman Catholic and Anglican traditions have, for instance, a discipline called moral theology.
2. Seward Hiltner, *Preface to Pastoral Theology* (Nashville, TN: Abingdon, 1958), p. 224. Hiltner attributes the first book on pastoral theology to C. T. Seidel, 1749.
3. *Catalogue of the Theological Seminary of the Presbyterian Church in the United States at Princeton, New Jersey,* January 1, 1821.
4. Hiltner offers a summary in *Preface to Pastoral Theology,* p. 224.
5. John T. McNeill, *A History of the Cure of Souls* (New York: Harper and Bros., 1951).
6. Hiltner, *Preface,* pp. 18–55.
7. James N. Lapsley, "Pastoral Theology: Past and Present," in *The New Shape of Pastoral Theology,* ed. W. B. Oglesby (Nashville, TN: Abington, 1969), p. 43.
8. James N. Lapsley, "Pastoral Theology: Its Nature, Methods, Uses," *The Princeton Seminary Bulletin* 1, 1 (New Series, 1977): 23.
9. Rodney J. Hunter, "The Future of Pastoral Theology," *Pastoral Psychology* 29, 1 (Fall 1980): 67.
10. Don Browning, "Pastoral Theology in a Pluralistic Age," *Pastoral Psychology* 29, 1 (Fall 1980): 32 ff. Also chapter 10 in this volume.
11. James N. Lapsley, *Salvation and Health: The Interlocking Processes of Life* (Philadelphia: Westminster, 1972).
12. Erik H. Erikson, *Childhood and Society* (New York: Norton, 1950); Jane Loevenger with the assistance of Augusto Blasi, *Ego Development: Conceptions and Theories* (San Francisco: Jossey-Bass, 1976).
13. Walter B. Cannon, *The Wisdom of the Body* (New York: Norton, 1939).
14. It must be said that the distinction between *psychē* and *pneuma* is not consistently maintained in the New Testament and that sometimes they are used interchangeably. Nevertheless, in many passages *pneuma* retains its dynamic transpersonal force in both human and divine life, for example, in Romans 8:9–26. The conception of spirit presented in this essay has been developed with particular debts to Daniel D. Williams's *The Spirit and the Forms of Love* (New York: Harper & Row, 1968) and to Reinhold Niebuhr's *The Nature and Destiny of Man* (New York: Scribner's, 1943), in their affirmation of spirit as concrete expression of human life in its capacity for self-transcendence and freedom, and their denial that it is either identical with *nous* or nearly so, and that it is a *donum superadditum*. I disagree with Niebuhr's radical disjuncture of spirit from nature, and find Williams's treatment, focused as it is upon one aspect of spirit, the interpersonal (p. 4), less than a satisfactory guide to the concept as a whole, while finding that his basic definition, ". . . the concrete personal expression of living creative beings" (p. 3), is congruent with my own understanding.
15. Silvan S. Tomkins, *Affect, Imagery, Consciousness,* Vol. 1, *The Positive Affects* (New York: Springer, 1962), p. 121.

10. Pastoral Theology in a Pluralistic Age

DON S. BROWNING

WHAT is the future of pastoral theology? In this chapter I advance a primarily theological and normative answer to this question. I do not speculate about the sociological fortunes of pastoral theology. Rather, I risk some vision of what pastoral theology *should* become if it were true to itself and true to that religious tradition which has evolved out of our Jewish and Christian heritage.

My present hopes for the future of pastoral theology are continuous with the view put forth in my *Moral Context of Pastoral Care*.[1] Pastoral theology should rediscover itself as a dimension of theological or religious ethics. It is the primary task of pastoral theology to bring together theological ethics and the social sciences to articulate a normative vision of the human life cycle. Pastoral theology involves stating the appropriate relation between a moral theology of the human life cycle and psychodynamic, developmental, and other social science perspectives that describe or explain how human development comes about.[2] In addition, pastoral theology should express a theology of those pastoral acts through which this normative vision of the human life cycle is appropriately mediated to individuals and groups in all of their situational, existential, and developmental particularity. Furthermore, pastoral theology in the future increasingly must express itself within a pluralistic society of diverse religio-cultural assumptions, differing cultural disciplines, and conflicting ethical patterns of life. In taking this position, I am in tension with perspectives developed in this book by James Lapsley and, to some extent, James Fowler.

Although this vision of pastoral theology can be stated rather simply, the overall project is exceedingly complex. There are, however, unique features to this proposal that may have productive consequences for the long-term health of both pastoral theology and the allied practices of pastoral care, pastoral counseling, and pastoral psychotherapy.

Interest in pastoral theology has languished behind interest and development in pastoral care, pastoral counseling, and pastoral psychotherapy. We have made advances in our technologies of intervention into such life-cycle issues as adolescence, sexuality, marriage, adulthood, aging, and death. But our normative theological visions of these milestones of the life cycle have received less and less of our attention. More and more, I fear, we have tried to intervene into these life-cycle issues with increasingly diffuse and confused normative theological images—images that should serve, when properly stated, as meaning contexts for our pastoral work. We borrow from the psychotherapeutic and developmental psychologies. But we are sometimes oblivious to the fact that we appropriate from them not only scientific information and therapeutic techniques but various normative visions of human fulfillment that are often neither philosophically sound nor theologically defensible.[3]

In the remainder of this chapter, I want to present an outline for a discipline of pastoral theology, or what could just as appropriately be called a practical theology of care (see Fig. 10.1). I will do this by pointing to the range of questions with which pastoral theology as a discipline should concern itself. To facilitate this, it will help to present the main facts of a pastoral case. It is a problem that calls for a pastoral response informed by both theological ethical and psychodynamic perspectives.

Mary Jones is a twenty-seven-year-old public school nurse. She has just made an appointment with a Protestant chaplain in a major metropolitan hospital. Although she is Roman Catholic, she has sought out a Protestant clergyman to get advice about the possibility of having an abortion. Mary has been married but has been divorced for slightly over one year. She has been employed for five years. When she got her divorce she returned to the city where she grew up and where her father and siblings reside. Her entire family is Roman Catholic. She has no plans to marry the father of her child. She was

Figure 10.1. The Place of Pastoral Theology (a Practical Theology of Care) Within the Context of the Other Theological Disciplines

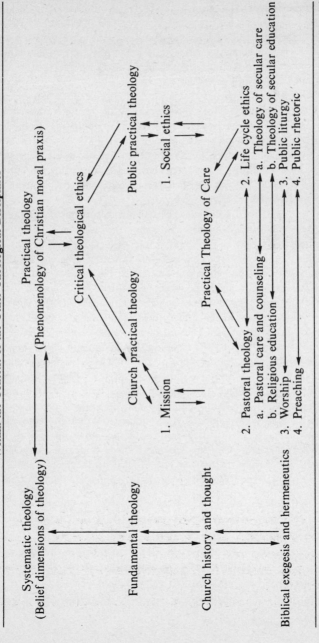

Note especially how practical theology is seen to be the organizing rubric for both theological ethics and the pastoral disciplines of missions, pastoral theology, religious education, and worship-preaching. Note as well that each of the church disciplines has a "public" counterpart which is also seen as part of the practical theological enterprise.

referred to the chaplain by her psychotherapist, who felt he was unable to help her make the decision about the abortion.

She believes that divorce, extramarital sex, and abortion all are sins. Yet she is somewhat attracted by the possibility of actually having the child. On the other hand, she wonders whether her traditional Catholic values will serve her well at this time.

The chaplain reported that a kind of cost-benefit analysis characterized her thought about the possibility of having an abortion. On the cost side, if she had the abortion she would (a) probably feel guilty, (b) lose a child which, in fact, she had always wanted, and (c) incur some health risks. On the benefit side, she would (a) not jeopardize her relationship with her family, (b) be free of the burden of raising a child, (c) not lose her nursing job, and (d) not incur other embarrassments.

The chaplain took note of this attempt to sort out her options, but he also made some inquiry into her developmental history. He learned that she was the oldest child of a lower-middle-class Irish Catholic family of three children. She remembers having strained relations with her mother as a young child. This appeared to be due to the jealousy that existed between herself and her younger sister for which her mother always held her responsible. Her mother died, however, when she was eleven years old. At that time a remarkable transformation came over her. She assumed the position of the head of the house. She did all of the cooking, cleaning, and other household work. Her father praised her for this profusely and she called her father the most "wonderful man in the world." She talked this way about her father in spite of the fact that he had a persistent problem with alcohol. After graduation, she went to nursing school and later married a medical student. Mary helped put her husband through medical school. The divorce came after her husband became established as a doctor and "seemed not to need or really appreciate her anymore." Having the baby would at least mean "having someone to take care of," and "someone who would appreciate her."

In contrast to the typical case discussed in the pastoral care literature where ethical issues are generally overlooked, the presenting problem is here clearly ethical. In addition, because Mary is already in therapy it is inappropriate for the chaplain to redefine the situation totally in the direction of the psychodynamic and motivational issues. Yet, I would contend that even to handle the ethical issues responsibly (consistent with the religio-ethical commitments of the Christian ministry), this chaplain should keep psychodynamic perspective in mind as horizon and background in his ethical considerations. The very essence of pastoral care is found in addressing the religio-ethical dimensions of human problems with an equal consideration for the dynamic-motivational issues as well.

I want to reflect on this case from a religious perspective, an ethical perspective, and a psychodynamic perspective—in that order. In doing this, I hope to outline the discipline of pastoral theology. It will be a hierarchical ordering of the issues of pastoral theology. By this I mean that the religious issues are fundamental (although not in all respects determinative) of the ethical and the psychodynamic issues. Even though this is true logically and methodologically, this does not necessarily mean that in all pastoral care cases the pastor must always place religious or ethical issues before psychodynamic ones. Care always entails a focus-ground structure. In some cases, psychodynamic issues should be in the foreground, but if the religious and ethical dimensions are in the background and the pastor knows how to articulate the way they are operative, the care and counseling being offered is nonetheless pastoral in the proper and full sense of the word.

The following propositions will, I hope, advance my point of view:

1. *Pastoral theology should be understood as philosophical reflection on the major themes of the Judeo-Christian tradition with special regard for the implication of these themes for a normative vision of the human life cycle.* It may be surprising to hear me refer to pastoral theology as a type of philosophical reflection. But to understand it in this way will have great clarifying consequences for a variety of pastoral care ministries, especially those ministries such as institutional chaplains or pastoral psychotherapists who must articulate their role before various professions and constituencies within the public world. It is difficult for chaplains to explain intelligibly to a doctor or social worker their role identity in narrowly confessional terms. It is better to articulate one's faith assumptions in a more public and philosophical language. And it is certainly better to do this rath-

er than lapsing, due to discomfort with narrowly confessional language, into the jargon of the social sciences as is the case with so many of our pastoral specialists today.

I am proposing here a revised correlational method of doing pastoral theology (practical theology of care) analogous to the revised correlational method proposed by David Tracy in the arena of fundamental theology.[4] This method is different from the Tillichian model which correlates questions from an analysis of existence with answers from Christian revelation.[5] The revised model critically correlates both questions and answers found in the Christian faith with questions and implied answers in various secular perspectives (the human sciences, the arts) on common human experience.[6] It is interesting to speculate on the similarities between the revised correlational model and the Hiltner-Williams model of "correlation of perspectives."[7] The Hiltner-Williams correlational method is closer to Tracy than it is to Tillich. The Hiltner-Williams model was basically a philosophical approach to pastoral theology. It certainly started with faith, but it brought the intuitions of faith into the public arena, fostered public discussion, reflected critically on the facts of faith, and attempted to advance publicly defensible reasons for the relevance of faith within the context of the public hospital, the public healing disciplines, and other public communities that are the context for our common lives.

The chaplain in this case should understand his task in a publicly and philosophically articulated way. If this chaplain chooses to guide this woman toward a particular attitude toward abortion, it will be better if he can defend his stand publicly, that is philosophically, even though the beginning point of his position may be grounded in faith. Here, as always, it should be faith seeking understanding. A purely confessional view of pastoral theology will no longer serve either the pastoral minister functioning increasingly within the context of a pluralistic and secular culture or the chaplain and pastoral psychotherapist who must function within various pluralistic (and therefore public) interdisciplinary contexts. This first point will become more clear as we complete our discussion of the following propositions.

2. *Pastoral theology must attempt to discern and articulate*

the relevance to care of both the religious dimension of common experience as well as the explicit faith themes of the historic Judeo-Christian tradition. This proposition follows directly from the first. If pastoral theology is to have a public character, it must concern itself with both the explicit themes of our historic faith as well as the tacit religious dimensions of everyday experience.

The desire to care for another person, whether it comes from a a minister or a secular therapist, presupposes certain attitudes of a religious kind. Deciding to care for another person assumes certain convictions that that person is worth valuing and caring for, not just for certain instrumental purposes, but intrinsically and with regard to some wider, if not ultimate, standard of value and worth. A variety of contemporary philosophers and theologians (Stephen Toulmin, David Tracy, Schubert Ogden, Bernard Lonergan, Paul Tillich) have argued that all of our finite judgments about both truth and value presupposed limit-experiences and a "limit-language" about wider measures of the true and the valuable.[8] David Tracy, following Lonergan, illustrates the function of limit-language in the area of scientific judgments. For the scientist to be rigorous and constantly open to the truth, he or she must ask such questions as "Can these answers work if the world is not intelligible? Can the world be intelligible if it does not have an intelligent ground?"[9] Tracy is suggesting that at the outer limits of the scientist's enterprise, there exist certain assumptions about the intelligibility of the world that are finally of a religious kind.

I believe that something similar exists in all acts of care. This, I feel, is what both Thomas Oden and I were getting at some fourteen years ago in our respective books entitled *Kerygma and Counseling* and *Atonement and Psychotherapy*.[10] Both of us believed we discerned a kind of limit-experience behind the attitude of acceptance that is fundamental to all good psychotherapies, even secular ones, regardless of their other differences.[11] We both argued that every specific attitude of therapeutic acceptance presupposed a deeper judgment about the ultimate acceptability of the person, not just to the therapist, but to some ultimate ground that bestows all value and assigns all acceptability.[12] We both believed that this limit-experience requires a "limit-language" to give expression to it (although we did not use this Tracy-Toulmin terminology in those days) and that religious language is precisely the language that serves that function. We differed, however, in that Oden insisted that only the symbols formed by the revelation of God in Jesus Christ (*Deus Pro Nobis*) provided this language,[13] whereas I insisted on a correlational method (maybe even a revised correlational method) that correlated our secular intuitions of this ground with the language of revelation.[14]

If pastoral theology can be philosophical enough to discern and articulate the limit-assumptions behind every act of care, pastoral practitioners can take their place more comfortably in the various pluralistic contexts that characterize contemporary ministry in both its specialized and generalized forms. Even this chaplain can profit from this bifocal perspective on his relation by Mary Jones. This chaplain may want to ground his care for her under the rubric of the love of God in Jesus Christ. But he also should be aware that this faith assumption is not altogether different from the limit-assumptions that secular therapists (even the therapist in this case) also make. Even the secular therapist must answer the question, why do I care for this person? Why is this person worth helping? Why am I obligated to help? These questions point to limit-assumptions that taper off into religious faith. The chaplain is fed by both sources of faith—those of common experience *and* explicit religious traditions. The difference between the minister and the secular therapist is not that one has faith and the other doesn't; it is rather that the minister has the additional resources of a specific religious tradition. Recognizing this fact makes it possible for the minister to take his or her place more gracefully in the contemporary pluralistic situation characterizing the helping disciplines today.

But the fuller task of pastoral theology is to give philosophical expression to the norms for the human life cycle explicitly found in the major themes of the Judeo-Christian tradition. Once again, it should be a matter of faith seeking understanding. Our task is to state the norms not just for the faithful (although certainly for them), but also to determine whether these norms have general public meaning, that is, whether they have general significance even for those who are not explicitly Christian. Is there something about Christian attitudes and norms of behavior that is valid for our mental health system, for our educational system, for our public policies with the aged and ill? Obviously, we cannot address these issues in the public arena from a narrowly confessional stance. This is why pastoral theology in the contemporary pluralistic situation should have an increasingly public and philosophical character.

3. *Pastoral theology should understand itself as an expression of theological ethics, primarily concerned with the religio-ethical norms governing the human life cycle.* This proposition is the most novel of the four that I am advancing and the one that signals most clearly the facet of pastoral theology being neglected today. Pastoral care is frequently seen as a religious enterprise, but we overlook the ways it is also an ethical enterprise. In this case, the situation is clear: this woman is asking for ethical guidance. Would most of our ministers, chaplains, and pastoral counselors know how to give it? Would they attempt to avoid the ethical issue and retreat to a psychodynamic reduction of her concerns? In this case, that would be doubly inappropriate since she already has her psychotherapist. Would one simply try to help her make a decision that she could live with and feel comfortable with? Once again, her therapist can also do this!

But how do we proceed? What are our ethical methodologies? Once again, a philosophical or moral-philosophical perspective may help us sort out our theological-ethical options and do so in such a way as to communicate our stance in a reasoned way to our pluralistic moral situation. First, what kind of ethical thinking is Mary herself doing? In spite of Mary's rather traditional religious convictions, her style of ethical thinking is anything but classically Catholic in character. Her cost-benefit analysis is clearly, in the terms of moral philosophy, a kind of teleological thinking. Teleological moral thinking, moral philosophers tell us, always tries to answer the question of what we should do by trying to determine which act will bring about the greatest amount of good over evil. The teleologist is always interested in consequences; the moral thing to do is that which will bring into reality the greatest amount of good consequences when good is given a nonmoral (although not immoral) meaning, such as when we use it to refer to good health, good music, good food, and good times.

At first glance, one might think that she is a teleologist of a specifically utilitarian kind. Mary in her cost-benefit analysis is trying to calculate the good over evil that will come about as a consequence of different courses of action. Utilitarians invariably get into just this kind of calculations. But Mary is not a utilitarian, as we will soon see. She is much closer to another kind of teleological thinking—an ethical egoist perspective, typical of so much of the ethical thinking in the contemporary cultural situation.[15]

Mary is not a utilitarian because she is not doing her calculations—her cost-benefit analysis—with the good of the larger community in mind. A utilitarian always does his or her calculations with the larger community in view, trying to determine which act or rule, if followed, will produce the greatest amount of good over evil for the largest number of people.[16] Mary is not doing this. Mary is doing her cost-benefit analysis in terms of the amount of good over evil that will accrue solely to herself. This is the kind of ethical thinking that a teleologist of the ethical egoist kind invariably ends up doing. We should be reminded that some ethical egoists do things that indirectly create good for others, but they always do them primarily because of the good that will come to them. Mary is an ethical egoist in that sense. Each of the values she is weighing has significance first of all for herself; as of yet, she has asked no questions about the welfare of her family, the larger society, or the child she may someday have. In terms of Lawrence Kohlberg's stages of moral development, Mary may be somewhere between stage two (the instrumental-hedonistic stage) and stage three (the conventional good-girl bad-girl orientation).[17]

The chaplain has enough ethical sophistication to know that his own point of view is considerably different from that of Mary Jones. Although a Protestant, he agrees with the classical Catholic position about the sanctity of life, even the life of the fetus in its earliest stages. He agrees on this issue with a group of contemporary ethicists, both Protestant and Catholic, such as Paul Ramsey, Germain Grisez, and John Noonan.[18] But he also believes that the Catholic position puts too much emphasis upon physical life. It overlooks the possibility that God may cherish other values such as the quality of life for both the child and the mother, social integrity, and the emotional and spiritual health of all concerned. In the formal terms of moral philosophy, the counselor's position, insofar as he was aware of having one, tended toward a mixed deontological and teleological position. Deontological approaches to ethics do not first of all try to determine the morally right by calculating consequences and estimating the amount of nonmoral good an act or rule will realize. Deontological approaches to ethics try to establish the right on some first principle or intuition that is deemed to be intrinsically and self-evidently moral independent of consequences. The divine command of God, Kant's categorical imperative, and existentialist appeals to authenticity are all examples, in their different ways, of deontological approaches. The chaplain's mixed position was deontological in that the sanctity of life was for him both a revelational and intuitive given; it was teleological, however, in that he felt that this value, although always central, must sometimes be balanced with other values as well.[19] The chaplain's position is close in some respects to the theological utilitarianism of the liberal Catholic thinker Daniel Callahan, since for the chaplain, ethical thinking involves balancing a variety of social and individual values. But it also is close to James Gustafson's position when he wrote the following words in response to Paul Ramsey's strong antiabortion stand: "Paul Ramsey rests his case ultimately on a theological basis; life is sacred because it is valued by God. Good theological point. But one can ask, what other things does God value in addition to physical life? e.g., qualitative aspects of life, etc."[20] Hence, the chaplain's position would allow for the possibility of abortion, but not on narrowly egoistic grounds.

This pastoral care situation, where abortion counseling is the primary focus, is used here only to illustrate a range of ethical issues that pastoral counselors have been ignoring. Many other situations and many other issues could have been used to make my point. But this illustration alone is sufficient to raise a host of important issues. How does the counselor now proceed? Does he take a thoroughly eductive approach and let her solve this problem within her own mixed ethical-egoist and conformist values? Does he try to move her closer to his own way of thinking? Is her developmental history important? Does he need to attend to her feelings, her motivations, and her psychological makeup? What kind of helping relation should he offer her? How do the religious perspectives discussed above affect this relationship? How does the ethical perspective just mentioned affect the relation? These questions carry us into the last sections of this chapter and the heart of pastoral care—the practical judgment involved in bringing these religious and ethical perspectives together with the particularities of her situation, the strengths and weaknesses of her personality, and the initiatives and responsibilities she is likely to sustain.

4. *Pastoral theology should be concerned with specifying the logic, timing, and practical strategies for relating theological-ethical and psychodynamic perspectives on human behavior.* The chaplain's ethical outlook led him to believe that either an abortion or having the child and putting it up for adoption were the most responsible courses of action open to her. At the same time, he ended his one-half hour interview believing that, for psychodynamic reasons, Mary Jones was strongly attracted to the idea of having the baby. But time was of the essence. A decision had to be made soon. He concluded the interview by offering to have two additional conversations. In these conversations he hoped to widen the range of her moral thinking so that she would begin to consider, in addition to her own needs, the needs of her unborn child, the needs of her family, and finally the needs of the larger society. In addition, he hoped to broaden her ethical thinking while at the same time attending to the complexities of her own developmental history.

On the moral level, the chaplain believed that there were strong arguments against having and keeping the child. Her status as a single parent, the unlikely possibility of getting assistance from her family, her lack of financial resources, the possible deleterious effects on the child of being raised without both a mother and father, and finally the growth-inhibiting consequences that having the baby would have on Mary's life, led the chaplain to take a dim view of this option. On the other hand he could morally justify both abortion or placing the child for adoption. Although he affirmed the sanctity of the unborn fetus, he saw great risks connected with the future well-being of the child is she were to have and keep the child. In addition, he held the conviction that modern society already had spawned too many alienated and emotionally deficient individuals and that the welfare of the social whole argues for either abortion or placing the child for adoption with a loving and stable family.

But there were indications, he thought, that Mary was deeply attracted to keeping the child. The chaplain's rapid scanning of her developmental history led him to hypothesize that Mary was a mildly narcissistic individual whose problems, although not grave, were prestructural in nature (located developmentally earlier than the oedipal conflict and the differentiation of the personality into ego, superego, and id). The chaplain felt that what seemed to be an oedipal relation between Mary and her father was probably superficial. Using the thought of Heinz Kohut,[21] he hypothesized that the real developmental issue was the prestructural narcissistic blows dealt to her self-esteem by her mother who constantly criticized her for mistreating her younger siblings. The father's later appreciation (accentuated by his own alcoholic and dependent needs) helped compensate somewhat for earlier narcissistic deficits. But having little understanding of what was really happening, Mary developed the strategy of enhancing her self-regard through taking care of others who needed her. This led, the chaplain thought, to an early marriage and her investment in the financial support of her husband's education. This same need might also, he believed, be behind her wish "to have a child."

All of this the chaplain held only tentatively. He did want to speak with her further. He hoped that in getting to know her better, he might gain a clearer idea about how to bring her moral discernment and her dynamic self-understanding into a closer relation. He did not aspire to take over the role now being occupied by her therapist, but he did want to promote both moral and psychological growth. At his next session, he planned to guide her into discussing her deeper feelings about the possibility of having the baby. If it emerges that having and keeping the baby does feed into her overdetermined needs to be wanted and depended upon, the chaplain then hoped to raise some carefully phrased questions designed to suggest additional moral possibilities. He would ask if she had thought about the welfare of the child, the strain it would place on her, and the possible long-term strains it might place upon society. At a later time, the chaplain was prepared to share simply and without airs of moral superiority his own moral views and the reasons he used to support them. In this way, he hoped to launch a process of moral inquiry that would at once be undogmatic in tone and dynamically sensitive to both the complexities of her developmental history as well as her level of moral thinking.

In the process of this inquiry, the chaplain hoped to offer Mary Jones a relation that was both accepting and morally serious. Both the acceptance and the moral seriousness had, for the chaplain, religious foundations. These religious foundations can be found both in certain limit-experiences in ordinary experience (Tracy, Toulmin, Browning, Lonergan) and the major themes of the Judeo-Christian tradition. The acceptance that the chaplain will offer, if authentic, will help meet some of the needs for narcissistic support that Mary Jones will require if she is to undergo the struggle to enlarge her moral horizons. This acceptance and the value for life that it will communicate is of a piece with the religious presuppositions about the sanctity of life fundamental to the chaplain's ethical perspective on abortion. But here, as is always the case, religious convictions do not in themselves determine the final outcome of ethical deliberation. Religious convictions provide a framework and limit-language for ethical deliberation. But ethical deliberation itself requires more specific calculations about the determinate goods and values at stake in the situation at hand.

It is not the purpose of this chapter to suggest that what the chaplain did, what he believed at the moral or ethical level, and how he rationalized his choices are either right or wrong. Nor am I saying that the chaplain should be conducting this moral inquiry alone. Ideally, this chaplain would have strong relations with the larger church. The larger church, as I indicated in the *Moral Context of Pastoral Care,* would function as a community of moral discourse and moral inquiry. The chaplain's ethical deliberations would be a part of and reinforced by the ethical deliberations of the larger Christian community. Ideally, Mary Jones herself also would be a part of this community and its moral discourse. Nonetheless, what I am saying is that the issues that the chaplain faced, the philosophical attitude that he brought to his deliberations, and his willingness to think about both ethical and psychodynamic concerns—all of this at least makes visible the agenda for pastoral theology in the future. If pastoral theology accepts this agenda, it will serve more fully and holistically human beings who live in a world that is increasingly more complex and pluralistic.

NOTES

1. Don Browning, *The Moral Context of Pastoral Care* (Philadelphia: Westminster 1976).
2. This definition of pastoral theology is broader than that advanced in *The Moral Context of Pastoral Care.* In this book I defined pastoral theology as the theology of pastoral acts of care and associated practical theology with the task of developing a moral theology of the human life cycle. I am now willing to define pastoral theology as dealing with both (a) a moral theology of the human life cycle and (b) a theology of pastoral acts of care. Practical theology I now associate with the larger task of writing theology from the perspective of action in contrast to belief, the latter being the major task of systematic theology. In this perspective theological ethics is a division of practical theology.
3. To give an analysis of the tacit theories of moral obligation implicit in various psychotherapeutic psychologies, I have found it helpful to apply William Frankena's categorization of different styles of ethical thinking. See his *Ethics* (Englewood Cliffs, NJ: Prentice-Hall, 1973), pp. 12–65. On the basis of his theory of virtue, one could argue that orthodox psychoanalysis contains an implicit "trait ethical egoist" theory of human fulfillment of a hedonic kind, that most of the humanistic theories (Maslow, Rogers, Perls) are "trait ethical egoist" of a nonhedonic kind, that Erikson is a "trait rule utilitarian," that most of the existentialists are "trait act deontologists," and that Kohlberg is a "trait rule deontologist."
4. David Tracy, *Blessed Rage for Order* (New York: Seabury, 1975), pp. 32–63.
5. Paul Tillich, *Systematic Theology,* Vol 1 (Chicago: University of Chicago Press, 1951), pp. 3–68.

6. Tracy, *Blessed Rage for Order*, pp. 45–47.
7. See Seward Hiltner, *Preface to Pastoral Theology* (Nashville, TN: Abingdon, 1957); Daniel Day Williams, *The Minister and the Care of Souls* (New York: Harper & Brothers, 1961).
8. Stephen Toulmin, *An Examination of the Place of Reason in Ethics* (Cambridge: Cambridge University Press, 1970), pp. 217–221; Tracy, *Blessed Rage for Order,* pp. 94–119; Schubert Ogden, *The Reality of God* (New York: Harper and Row, 1963), p. 30; Bernard Lonergan, *Method in Theology* (New York: Herder and Herder, 1972), pp. 235–245; Paul Tillich, *Systematic Theology,* Vol 32, pp. 204–10.
9. Tracy, *Blessed Rage for Order,* p. 98.
10. Thomas Oden, *Kerygma and Counseling* (Philadelphia: Westminster, 1966); Don Browning, *Atonement and Psychotherapy,* (Philadelphia: Westminster, 1966).
11. Browning, *Atonement and Psychotherapy,* pp. 94–127.
12. Oden, *Kerygma and Counseling,* p. 21; Browning, *Atonement and Psychotherapy,* pp. 149–161.
13. Oden, *Kerygma and Counseling,* p. 63.
14. Browning, *Atonement and Psychotherapy,* pp. 149–173.
15. Frankena, *Ethics,* pp. 17–19.
16. *Ibid.,* p. 34.
17. Lawrence Kohlberg, "From Is to Ought," *Cognitive Development and Epistemology,* ed. Theodore Mischel (New York: Academic, 1971), p. 168.
18. Paul Ramsey, "Reference Points in Deciding About Abortion," *The Morality of Abortion,* ed. John T. Noonan (Cambridge, MA: Harvard University Press, 1970), 60–100; German Grisez, *Abortion: The Myths, The Realities, and the Arguments* (New York: Corpus Books, 1970); John T. Noonan, Jr., "An Almost Absolute Value in History," *The Morality of Abortion,* ed. John T. Noonan, Jr., pp. 1–59.
19. The possibility of a mixed deontological and teleological ethics is explained by William Frankena in his *Ethics,* p. 52.
20. As quoted in Daniel Callahan, *Abortion: Law, Choice, and Morality* (New York: Macmillan, 1970), p. 311.
21. Heinz Kohut, *The Analysis of the Self* (New York: International Universities Press, 1971).

Index